GILES TERERA MBE

Giles Terera MBE is an award-winⁱ

He trained at Mountview Theatre School and has worked consistently at venues such as the National Theatre, the Royal Shakespeare Company and Shakespeare's Globe. He is best known for originating the role of Aaron Burr in the West End production of the award-winning musical *Hamilton*, for which he won the 2018 Olivier Award for Best Actor in a Musical.

His other theatre credits include *Rosmersholm*, *The Tempest*, *Avenue Q*, *The Book of Mormon*, *125th Street*, *Rent* (West End); *Ma Rainey's Black Bottom*, *Hamlet*, *Death and the King's Horseman*, *The Hour We Knew Nothing of Each Other*, *Troilus and Cressida*, *Candide*, *Honk!* (National Theatre); *The Merchant of Venice* (Shakespeare's Globe/international tour); *The Resistible Rise of Arturo Ui* (Donmar Warehouse); *Pure Imagination – The Songs of Lesley Bricusse* (St. James's); *King John* (Shakespeare's Globe/UK tour); *Don't You Leave Me Here* (West Yorkshire Playhouse); *The Playboy of the Western World* (Abbey, Dublin); *The Ratpack* (West End/international tour); *Jailhouse Rock* (Theatre Royal Plymouth/West End); *You Don't Kiss* (Stratford Circus); *Up on the Roof* (Chichester); *The Tempest* (RSC); *Six Degrees of Separation* (Sheffield); *Generations of the Dead* (Young Vic); *Bill Shakespeare's Italian Job* (Playbox, Warwick/Gilded Balloon, Edinburgh); *The Demon Headmaster/The Animals of Farthing Wood* (Pleasance, Edinburgh).

As a writer, his theatre work includes *The Meaning of Zong* (Bristol Old Vic/BBC Radio 3), *The Ballad of Soho Jones* (St. James's) and *Black Matter* (Crazy Coqs). As a filmmaker, Giles's first documentary, *Muse of Fire* – created with Dan Poole – centres on modern perspectives of Shakespeare and premiered on BBC Four in Autumn 2013. Giles was an associate producer on Poole's feature documentary *The Space: Theatre of Survival*, and he wrote and directed the concert film *Hello Harry! A Celebration*. His book, *Hamilton and Me: An Actor's Journal*, was published by Nick Hern Books in 2021 and featured as BBC Radio 4 Book of the Week.

Giles was appointed a Member of the Order of the British Empire (MBE) in the 2020 New Year Honours for services to theatre.

Other Titles in This Series

Giles Terera

THE MEANING OF ZONG

NICK HERN BOOKS
London
www.nickhernbooks.co.uk

A Nick Hern Book

The Meaning of Zong first published in Great Britain in 2022 as a paperback original by Nick Hern Books Limited, The Glasshouse, 49a Goldhawk Road, London W12 8QP

The Meaning of Zong copyright © 2022 Giles Terera

Giles Terera has asserted his right to be identified as the author of this work

Cover image: Josiah Hyacinth

Designed and typeset by Nick Hern Books, London
Printed in Great Britain by Mimeo Ltd, Huntingdon, Cambridgeshire PE29 6XX

A CIP catalogue record for this book is available from the British Library

ISBN 978 1 83904 029 0

'Ships at a distance have every man's wish on board.'
Zora Neale Hurston, *Their Eyes Were Watching God*

The play is dedicated to
Brian Haw,
Daniel Weyman,
Michael Balogun
and Anni Domingo

Author's Note
Giles Terera

I didn't read about the story of *The Zong*. I didn't learn of it
from a documentary. A friend of mine, Anni Domingo, told me
about it. I could trace that moment all the way back to Olaudah
Equiano telling the story to Granville Sharp two hundred years
earlier. For this reason I knew that this story would be best told
in the theatre, which of all mediums has the greatest potential
for a relationship between performers who are telling the story
and audience who are receiving it.

It is not a play about good black people and bad white people; it
is a story about people. One of the things which drew me to the
story as a possible piece of theatre is that it contained such a
diverse group of characters. Productions should observe this in
casting. The play is intended to be an ensemble piece of theatre
for a company of twelve.

Music should be present throughout the play. The words to 'The
Song of Unforgetting' were created by myself for the BBC
Radio 3 production and then added to by Sidiki Dembele for
our original theatrical production. The words to the song are:

Listen!
Remember.
Do not worry, remember.

The song is made up by the characters on the spot, so the
music/melody should be simple and efficient.

Much of what is said by the officials in the play is taken
verbatim from the legal proceedings at Westminster Hall and
various correspondence left to us by Granville Sharp and
Olaudah Equiano.

Many people have added to the journey of this play. Specifically
during the many workshops and readings we held during its
development. I am grateful to each of them, especially Tom
Morris.

The Meaning of Zong was first performed at Bristol Old Vic on 7 April 2022 (previews from 2 April), with the following cast:

OTTOBAH CUGOANO	Michael Elcock
GRANVILLE SHARP	Paul Higgins
SIR JOHN LEE /	
ROBERT STUBBS /	
WILLIAM WOODFALL	Simon Holland-Roberts
ARTHUR PIGOTT /	
JAMES KELSALL	Remi King
AMA / GLORIA	Kiera Lester
JOYI / LORD MANSFIELD	Bethan Mary-James
ANNIE GREENWOOD /	
ELIJAH BROWN	Eliza Smith
OLAUDAH EQUIANO	Giles Terera
RIBA	Alice Vilanculo
ONSTAGE MUSICAL	
DIRECTOR	Sidiki Dembele

All other parts played by members of the company

Writer	Giles Terera
Directors	Giles Terera and Tom Morris
Set and Costume Designer	Jean Chan
Composer and	
Musical Director	Sidiki Dembele
Sound Designer and	
Co-Composer	Dave Price
Lighting Designer	Zeynep Kepekli
Video Designer	Tom Newell
	of Limbic Cinema
	with Will Duke
Movement Director	Ingrid Mackinnon
Assistant Director	Nadia Williams
Costume Supervisor	Rhianne Good
Dramatherapist	Samantha Adams

Beatbox and Loop Coach	Conrad Murray
Fight Director	Kate Waters
Associate Directors	Julia Head and Claire O'Reilly
Production Manager	Ed Wilson
Company Stage Manager	Emily Walpole
Deputy Stage Manager	Fiona Bardsley
Assistant Stage Manager	Eve Richardson
Stage Management Placement	Grace Dobson

An earlier version of the play was broadcast on BBC Radio 3 on 21 March 2021, produced by Jonx Productions in collaboration with Bristol Old Vic, as part of BBC Lights Up, with Giles Terera as Olaudah Equiano and Samuel West as Granville Sharp, directed by Tom Morris.

Characters

OLAUDAH EQUIANO/GUSTAVUS VASSA, *a barber*
GRANVILLE SHARP, *a music teacher*
ANNIE GREENWOOD, *a teacher*
OTTOBAH CUGOANO, *an abolitionist*
AMA/GLORIA, *an artist*
RIBA, *a teacher*
JOYI, *a mother*
LORD MANSFIELD, *Lord Chief Justice of Great Britain*
SIR JOHN LEE, *a lawyer*
ARTHUR PIGOTT, *a lawyer*
WILLIAM WOODFALL, *a newpaper publisher*
ROBERT STUBBS, *a passenger*
ELIJAH BROWN, *a sailor*
JAMES KELSALL, *first mate*
SHOP ASSISTANT
BOOKSHOP MANAGER
THE BISHOP OF CHESTER
BOY
DOCK OFFICER
GAOLER
CLERKS
MICHAEL, *a sailor*
GEORGE, *a sailor*
JOHN, *a sailor*

Note

A 'shudder' is a sonic representation of a character's feeling, in response to something they've heard or remembered.

This text went to press before the end of rehearsals and so may differ slightly from the play as performed.

Scene One

Bookshop. Present day. Late afternoon. GLORIA *stops a* SHOP ASSISTANT.

GLORIA. Excuse me? Do you work here?

SHOP ASSISTANT. How can I help?

GLORIA. This book – it was in the wrong section.

ASSISTANT. Sorry? Oh – right, yeah, people will put them back in the wrong places –

GLORIA. I don't mean someone put it back in the wrong place.

ASSISTANT. Sorry?

GLORIA. Thought I was going blind. It said online you had a copy in stock.

ASSISTANT. Can I see...? (*Looks at the book.*) Okay, thanks. Should've been over there in the Africa section.

GLORIA. It was.

ASSISTANT. So it was in the right section.

GLORIA. No.

ASSISTANT. I don't – (*Scans the blurb.*) '*Empire of Chains*: The true story of the voyage which led to abolition.' Ah, sorry, with you now. Yes, it's supposed to be in the slavery section.

GLORIA. Which is in the Africa section.

ASSISTANT. ...Which is where you found it.

GLORIA. Yeah.

ASSISTANT. So... it *was* in the right section.

GLORIA. No.

TANNOY ANNOUNCEMENT. Ladies and gentlemen, the shop will be closing in two minutes. Please make your way to the checkout. Thank you.

MANAGER. Is everything all right, Sharon?

ASSISTANT. Yeah. This lady –

GLORIA. Noticed that you have this book in the wrong section.

MANAGER. Let's have a look? (*Reads*.) '*Empire of Chains*'. Just out. Yeah – it should be over here in African history –

ASSISTANT. Like I said.

GLORIA. It *was* over there in African history.

MANAGER. I thought you said someone put in the wrong place.

GLORIA. I did.

MANAGER. So how can it be in the wrong place?

GLORIA. Maybe you should ask whoever decides the layout of the store.

MANAGER. I do.

GLORIA. So...?

MANAGER. I'm sorry I don't – if it shouldn't be in the Africa section where should it be?

GLORIA. There.

MANAGER. That's the British history section.

GLORIA. Right.

ASSISTANT. Kevin... I think I should see to these custo–

MANAGER. Just a sec – it's about slavery. No?

GLORIA. The British slave trade.

MANAGER. That's what I said.

GLORIA. You said slavery. This book's about a British trade, a British institution. Created by the British. Benefited from by the British. Therefore the correct place for this would be...?

MANAGER. But... carried out on *Africans* –

GLORIA. By the British.

MANAGER. Absolutely. Look, I'm an ally. We didn't actually have a slavery section before. Obviously since George Floyd we wanted –

GLORIA. George Floyd? I'm talking about the British slave trade.

MANAGER. I get what you're saying –

GLORIA. Do you?

MANAGER. Totally. It's just… Look, if it were up to me –

GLORIA. You said it was up to you. Mate, you seem like a cool guy. You say you're an ally. Respectfully I say to you – prove it. I'm sure you went on the BLM marches, took a knee, but now what?… What would happen if you – *you* took this book and put it in the middle of that shelf? Between King George III and Queen Victoria.

TANNOY. Ladies and gentlemen, the shop is now closed, please make your way to the checkouts.

ASSISTANT. Kevin…

MANAGER. I'm more than happy to forward your complaint to head office –

GLORIA. Not a complaint – the truth.

MANAGER. Jot it down on an email and I'll pass it on –

GLORIA. You won't do it, will you? Why?

MANAGER. If you wanna purchase the book I can put that through for you. Otherwise we are closed I'm afraid. (*Goes.*)

GLORIA. Exactly. You're afraid. Can't even give me a proper reason.

OLAUDAH. Not the reason, the response.

GLORIA (*starts*). Sorry?

OLAUDAH. Remember?

GLORIA. Remember what? Do I know you?

OLAUDAH. Wait for white people to put it there, you'll be waiting a long time.

GLORIA. Who are you?

OLAUDAH. You know. The one in that book. (*Extends a hand*.) Olaudah.

GLORIA. Equiano?

OLAUDAH. Correct.

GLORIA. Sure. I'm losing it.

OLAUDAH. Page one hundred and thirty-two.

She stares then flips pages. As she does –

European scientists might try and find some equation for my presence but you and I call it… Life. Anansi can be spider *and* human. A piece of rope can be God's finger. I lived long ago but I am here for you, just as you helped me two hundred years ago.

GLORIA. I didn't help you –

OLAUDAH. *Think*, Gloria.

GLORIA. How do you know my name? How could I have –

OLAUDAH. You are a Black woman, you can do All Things. Last paragraph.

GLORIA. 'One detail however which we know for certain is that, miraculously, one of the Africans did in fact survive… – '

OLAUDAH. You. You stand before me because someone chose to survive. That you rise.

GLORIA. Okay, I get it. But I'm not talking concepts, what I'm saying is what do we *do*? This guy – (*Re: the* MANAGER.)

OLAUDAH. Can't answer you because he answers to his boss, who answers to her boss, who answers to their board. That's the fight. We were afraid. But still we fought.

GLORIA. Things are different now.

OLAUDAH. Are they?

Thunder.

Are they indeed?

He throws the book up and its leaves explode and scatter, transforming our setting from the twenty-first to the eighteenth century.

This is a true story.

Rain. Music.

1783.

COMPANY. Britain's just lost the war –

COMPANY. George III surrenders to Washington – therefore –

COMPANY. America is born with a gun in its hand –

COMPANY. Britain – is fucked but determined to stand –

COMPANY. New empires –

COMPANY. Technology –

COMPANY. Media –

COMPANY. The modern world appears
A world on fire with explosive ideas

Mozart writing hits
Turner painting ships
Young Napoleon's at military school picking up tips

A new century
A new time
The Age of Enlightenment
Eighteenth century

Royal Africa Company – BOOM!
East India Company – BOOM!
A golden age for banks and profiteers
That's sweet music to European ears
Business is booming – everyone cheers.

OLAUDAH. And it is human slavery which greases the gears.

I'm in London. On Granville Sharp's doorstep. That night
I knocked – I was someone else. This story showed me who
I am and what I must do.

(*Hammering desperately on the door.*) Mister Sharp!

He is now 'VASSA'.

GRANVILLE. Who is it?

VASSA. Granville Sharp?!

GRANVILLE. What is it?

VASSA. Hello…?!

GRANVILLE. I'm busy –

VASSA. Please! Please!!

GRANVILLE. Wait… (*Opens the door.*) Who are you?

VASSA. Gustavas Vassa.

GRANVILLE. Come in. Come in. Shoes.

As VASSA *removes his shoes,* GRANVILLE *fetches some papers.*

You're the first one here in some time. I can help you but I'll need the name of your owner.

VASSA. Gustavus Vassa.

GRANVILLE.…Then who is it you are running from?

VASSA. I've not come for my freedom, Mister Sharp. That is mine.

GRANVILLE. Why have you come?

VASSA. Your letter –

GRANVILLE. What letter?

VASSA. In the *Morning Chronicle*. The killings.

GRANVILLE. Killings?

VASSA. One word you used, I don't understand it – '*Shudder*'.

GRANVILLE. I'm sorry?

VASSA. It means something like quake, no? To shudder. I have been in earthquakes.

GRANVILLE. What do you mean?

VASSA. In the paper. Or is it closer to shiver? But shiver is to do with cold, no?

GRANVILLE. I don't know what you're talking about.

VASSA. You are Granville Sharp?

GRANVILLE. But I wrote no letter to the *Chronicle*.

VASSA. Yes.

GRANVILLE. No.

VASSA. Yes. You must have.

GRANVILLE. Why?

VASSA. Because Granville Sharp is the only one in Britain who gives a damn about Black people. They say. My hands. I can't stop.

GRANVILLE. You should go.

VASSA. My hands... drowned... They killed her.

GRANVILLE. Killed? Who?

VASSA. – In the water. Threw her in – from – . A child. Why did they throw children, Mister Sharp?

GRANVILLE. Who?

VASSA. On the... the...

GRANVILLE. Who? Where?... Where...?! Unless you say, I cannot help.

VASSA. Ship. The ship... –

GRANVILLE. Where?

VASSA. Caribbean.

GRANVILLE. You saw this?

VASSA. I read it.

GRANVILLE. Where?

VASSA. Your letter!

VASSA *thrusts the paper at him.* GRANVILLE *takes a breath and reads.*

GRANVILLE. 'Sir, on the 6th I heard an insurance trial at the Guildhall. An action had been brought against the underwriters of a British slave ship out of Liverpool to recover from their insurers the value of one hundred and thirty-two African slaves thrown overboard and drowned in the passage from Africa to Jamaica, of which these were the circumstances:

Before Lord Chief Justice Mansfield it was claimed that, during the middle passage from Africa, navigational errors led to a want of water aboard the ship, whereupon reaching the Caribbean the captain Luke Collingwood or his first mate James Kelsall ordered the crew to first select forty-six of the women slaves from the hold and throw them handcuffed into the sea to drown.'

VASSA *hears the following voices.* GRANVILLE *does not.*

AMA. forty-six

GRANVILLE. 'Two days later thirty-six male slaves were thrown overboard.'

RIBA. thirty-six

GRANVILLE. 'The following day forty more Negroes were drowned.'

JOYI. forty

GRANVILLE. 'Ten other slaves, fearing the same fate as their countrymen jumped in after these and were drowned along with them.'

RIBA. ten

GRANVILLE. 'One child was thrown into the sea. One African survived. The narrative seemed to make every person in the court *shudder* – '

VASSA. forty-six... thirty-six...

AMA (*overlapping*). forty-six... thirty-six...

GRANVILLE. ' – and I waited expecting the jury to apply to the court for information how to bring the perpetrators to justice. No such plea was made.'

VASSA. forty... ten...

JOYI (*overlapping*). forty... ten...

GRANVILLE. 'Instead with only one witness – a passenger; Robert Stubbs – and without going out of court the jury found in favour of the ship's owners in Liverpool who are to be awarded three thousand, nine hundred and sixty pounds for the one hundred and thirty-two slaves they drowned.'

RIBA. One hundred and thirty-two

VASSA. One hundred and thirty-two.

AMA. One child...

GRANVILLE....Mister Vassa?

RIBA....was thrown into the sea.

GRANVILLE. Mister Vassa?

VASSA *is jolted back into the room.*

VASSA. I – I'm –

GRANVILLE (*shaken*)....I didn't write this.

VASSA....What?...

GRANVILLE. I have fought slavery twenty years. Alone. I never heard anything like this. I didn't write it.

VASSA (*coming to*)....I have made a fool of myself.

GRANVILLE. Sit.

VASSA. I thought it was you. Forgive me.

GRANVILLE. Let me help you.

VASSA. You can't.

GRANVILLE. Justice must be done.

VASSA (*grabs the paper*). Forget it.

GRANVILLE. What? Give me that.

VASSA. You were not the one in that court.

GRANVILLE. Things would have been different if I were, I can assure you.

VASSA. You weren't. They aren't. So... (*Leaving.*)

GRANVILLE. What are you saying? One hundred and thirty-two people are dead!

VASSA. And I'm alive. You've no idea. Forget it. You're not... You think...

GRANVILLE. Calm yourself –

VASSA. I didn't come here for this –

GRANVILLE. Why did you come?

VASSA. Because your letter, or what I thought was your letter, shuddered me. And I don't want any more trouble. (*Taking the paper... screwing it up.*) Sorry to trouble you.

GRANVILLE. Of course not, all the Blacks come to me. Why should you be any different?

VASSA (*stopping*)....What?

GRANVILLE. All the Blacks come to me. Why would you be any different?

Beat.

VASSA. You don't know me. I came in and you assumed I was a runaway slave like the others. I am not like the others. My name is Gustavus Vassa. Named for a Swedish king. I bought my freedom from a British captain. Baptised. Studied my Scripture. Educated. I am a barber. I cut gentlemen's hair. Which I learned fighting this country's wars. Cutting Sir Thomas Hart's hair this evening as he was talking about our defeat in America I read the paper over his shoulder and saw this. He didn't see it. I did. My hands started shaking. I held the razor at his throat and my hands would not stop shaking. Your letter almost made a murderer of me –

GRANVILLE. It wasn't my letter, man, and you didn't commit murder. For murder is sin, is it not?

VASSA. Yes.

GRANVILLE. And does the Scripture not tell us that – to not answer sin is itself a sin?

VASSA. It does.

GRANVILLE. Well then?

VASSA. You said you were busy earlier? Writing I see.

GRANVILLE. Yes.

VASSA. What?

GRANVILLE. A book.

VASSA. Concerning? Music? Shakespeare?

GRANVILLE. I –

VASSA. You are known for both I know.

GRANVILLE. Biblical grammar if you must know –

VASSA. Grammar?

GRANVILLE. Classical grammar. Scripture translation from the Greek to English. I believe I have discovered a new principle –

VASSA. Then I will leave you to your commas and full stops.

GRANVILLE (*stunned*). Very well then. (*Picking up the paper.*) Go. Plainly you are not like all the others. Free. As a bird.

VASSA. You do not know me –

GRANVILLE. You go to sleep. But I go to justice.

GRANVILLE *tries to piece events together as* VASSA *collects his shoes.*

This makes no sense. Ship leaves Africa, crosses the Atlantic, gets lost. How? And this single commercial passenger. On a slave ship? I cannot imagine what happened to cause this –

VASSA *hears* AMA, GRANVILLE *does not. Neither man can see her.*

AMA. You can.

VASSA. What do you want?

AMA. You *can* imagine.

VASSA (*hearing but afraid*)....Stop...

AMA. Voices?

VASSA. Stop.

AMA. Visions...?

VASSA (*resisting*)....Yes...

SHUDDER.

We are suddenly at a chaotic Annamaboe Slave Port in Ghana, West Coast Africa. Ferocious sun and the din of the factory of humans.

...The fort. Ocean. The great boat. People. Chained. A pile of dead bodies in the surf. Sea birds pick from a baby. And white men, who sound even stranger than they look.

AMA (*to* VASSA)....in the shadow of...

VASSA....An enormous tree ...

ELIJAH BROWN *brings* RIBA *and* JOYI *to a standstill at the trunk of the tree. Followed by* KELSALL, *a* TRADER, *and* STUBBS.

KELSALL (*pointing out* JOYI *to the* TRADER). Pregnant. Too risky. Throw that one in – (*Re:* AMA.) and I'll take all three.

The deal is done.

(*Addressing the Africans.*) My name is Colonel Kelsall. You are now property of Mister William Gregson, the Christian Englishman who owns *that* ship... and every last one of you.

GRANVILLE. What happened between Africa and Jamaica?

KELSALL. I fucking hate Africa. As does Captain Collingwood. But today, finally, we leave and won't have to see it again for another year. *You* however shall never see it again.

AMA (*to* RIBA). Please? What is he saying?

RIBA. They are taking us. Shhh.

AMA. No.

JOYI. Quiet.

KELSALL. You want to stay alive. I want you alive. Do as you
are told and you'll live. Time is money, Stubbs, Gregson has
paid good money for these and expects a fuller profit from
them in the Caribbean than his last shipment. (*Gestures to
the tree*.) So let's have this thing over with, get these last
ones onboard and set sail.

STUBBS (*swatting flies*). Uh-uh-uh. Hold your horses,
sunshine. I don't work for you like the rest of these bastards
– (*Re: sailors*.)

KELSALL. What?

STUBBS. Don't forget I'm a passenger now. Civilian. Guest.
You have to be nice to me.

AMA. What are they saying?

JOYI. Shhh!!

KELSALL (*grabs* STUBBS *by the collar*). Now you listen to
me, I don't know who the fuck you are or how you managed
to become governor of this port but I do know that for
London to kick you out so soon and order your immediate
return you must be either a real failure or a real cunt. I am
guessing both. Now then, Former Governor/Failure/Cunt,
may I also remind you that you are the reason these people
are here in the first place. A fact I am sure they are all well
aware of. So if I were you I would shut your mouth and do
exactly as I tell you because between here and London I am
the only thing stopping any one of four hundred pairs of
Black hands reaching your failure/cunt throat. Do you
understand me? Now get on with this before I knock you out.

STUBBS (*immediately turns to* AMA). You. See this tree? Go
around it. Around the tree. Now. Move!

AMA (*to* RIBA). What does he say?

STUBBS (*to* AMA). You. (*Gestures*.) Move. Around the tree.
Seven times. Men – nine. Now! Walk round this tree seven
times.

AMA (*to* RIBA). What's happening?

JOYI. They want us to forget.

RIBA. It's a ritual.

AMA. What?

STUBBS. Move around the tree. Seven times. Do it!

KELSALL. Stubbs, do not test me.

JOYI. They call it the Tree of Forgetting.

AMA. Forget?

JOYI. Who we are. Our names. Where we came from. Our identity. History. Everything. I've seen them make every one of us do it before –

AMA. Why?

STUBBS. Bitch, do not test me.

RIBA. It means nothing. Do it.

AMA. I don't want to forget my name.

STUBBS (*to* RIBA). You understand English?

RIBA. Yes.

STUBBS. Tell her move around the tree.

RIBA. She just arrived. Doesn't understand.

KELSALL. I lose time, Stubbs.

STUBBS (*to* AMA). Do it. I lose time.

AMA. What is this?!

STUBBS (*cocks his pistol*). I don't give a shit. (*Places his pistol at* AMA's *temple*.)

RIBA (*to* AMA). Stay alive.

AMA. Somebody help us! Please!!

VASSA (*as if in a dream*)....Yes.

AMA *raises her foot and... steps. Cries out.*

SHUDDER.

Then AMA *places the other foot. Walks. When they come to a standstill –*

STUBBS. *Wasn't so hard. Again.* Good. No home. No name. No family. No Africa. No nothing.

STUBBS *steps up to* AMA.

Pretty thing. Don't you die. I'll need you during this voyage. Only unspoiled one left. (*To* KELSALL.) All yours, sunshine.

The whistle sounds and they are moved to the ship.

BROWN. Food at ten bells and four, between which time you remain below, except noon when Captain Collingwood permits you on deck to dance. From here to Jamaica it's nothing but sharks. Safest place for you is on this ship. Men – there. Women – there. Move it!

Africans sing 'The Song of Unforgetting'. BROWN *sings 'Tommy's Gone to Hilo'.*

As they move down the beach to the water and The Zong, AMA *hisses to* RIBA.

AMA. They believe in this ritual?

JOYI. The white man *lives* by ritual.

AMA. My name is Ama Owba. My father is Ndori of the Anyi. I am an artist.

JOYI. I am Joyi. See, it does not work. We did not forget.

AMA. Someone is coming to help us. I feel it.

RIBA. Or we must help ourselves. We must reach the men.

AMA. These white men fight –

RIBA. We will kill them before sunset and free ourselves –

JOYI. We are going, Ama.

AMA. Why his this happening? (*Vomits.*) Auntie, I cannot swim.

RIBA. Listen to me. I do not know exactly what awaits us but I know it will be bad. If you remember nothing else, remember this – you come from a land where the mountains are Great, the animals Strong and the people Ancient. Remember.

We are jolted back to GRANVILLE*'s house.*

GRANVILLE. I'll find them. If it takes another twenty years.

Beat.

VASSA. A week.

GRANVILLE. Sorry?

VASSA. They'll be at Westminster Hall next week.

Leafs through the paper and hands a new page to GRANVILLE.

GRANVILLE (*reads*). 'Gregson vs Gilbert. Westminster Hall. Maritime insurance appeal. Motion for *retrial*. Claim: Losses at sea.' This is them?

VASSA. Gregson is the owner, Gilbert the insurer. The owners won but the insurers are appealing the judgment. Monday.

GRANVILLE (*tearing off and folding the page*). 'For the love of money is the root of all evil.'

VASSA. One Timothy. Chapter Six.

GRANVILLE. Westminster Hall next week. We discover what happened. Meantime, we enquire at the admiralty tomorrow about prosecution.

VASSA. We?

GRANVILLE. We haven't much time.

VASSA. I can't... –

GRANVILLE. You can. Go to the docks then. Sailors talk. Try and find this Stubbs. The crew.

VASSA. How?

GRANVILLE. Same way you found me. (*Beat.*) Please.

AMA. Please.

VASSA *finds himself nodding.*

GRANVILLE. Good.

VASSA. You look scared.

GRANVILLE. So do you.

VASSA. Why are you scared?

Beat.

GRANVILLE. The first Negro who knocked on that door was called Jonathan Strong. Twenty years ago. I helped him gain freedom from his master and felt like I was changing the world. Yet for every one I've helped since, ten thousand more are taken. I fear I find myself in a world in which it is easier to prove a grammatical principle than it is to prove that slavery is a sin.

VASSA. 'I will lift up mine eyes unto the hills from whence cometh my strength.'

GRANVILLE. 'My strength cometh from the Lord.' You're a good man, Gustavus Vassa.

VASSA. As are you, Mister Sharp.

GRANVILLE. Granville.

VASSA. Granville. (*Turns to leave.*)

GRANVILLE. What's the name of this ship?

VASSA. *The Zong.*

Scene Two

A split scene: GRANVILLE *at the admiralty and* VASSA *at the docks.*

COMPANY (*to us*). While Gustav Vassa heads out early to the dock –

COMPANY. Granville Sharp attacks the admiralty hoping to shock –

COMPANY. But there he's passed from pillar to post, his target unassailable –

COMPANY. Finally informed that their lordships are all –

CLERK. Unavailable. The war. May I help?

GRANVILLE. I doubt it.

VASSA. Excuse me.

BROWN (*drunk*). Watch it, chief.

CLERK. What does it concern?

GRANVILLE. Their lordships.

BROWN. Here, give us a song. Your lot can sing as sweet as ever I heard.

He grabs VASSA *and twirls him around.*

CLERK. You have an appointment?

GRANVILLE. No.

CLERK. Then unfortunately –

VASSA. I am looking for men who may have been on the slave ship *Zong*. Do you know it?

BROWN. Know a lot of things.

GRANVILLE. Three hours I've been here. Murder charges. Correct procedure?

CLERK. Is by appointment.

GRANVILLE. Did you not hear me? I said murder charges.

VASSA. There was a murder.

CLERK/BROWN. Murder?

GRANVILLE. One hundred and thirty-two slaves. The correct procedure for criminal prosecution?

CLERK. As in… Negroes?

GRANVILLE. Correct.

VASSA. You've heard of it?

BROWN. 'For what doth it profit a man...'

CLERK. You're here –

BROWN. '...To gain the whole world and forfeit his soul.'

CLERK. Because someone has killed a Negro?

GRANVILLE. Are you deaf?

CLERK. Mister Shaw –

GRANVILLE. Sharp.

CLERK. Quite. His lordship Admiral Howe has only this week returned to Britain from the American conflict under the gravest possible circumstances to report to the prime minister and His Majesty on the outcome of the most regrettable situation in this nation's history and you come here expecting him to concern himself with a *dead Negro*?

GRANVILLE. Yes.

BROWN throws up into the water.

CLERK. Then may I say to you, sir, that you are a bloody disgrace. Next!

COMPANY (*to us*). Next: the bishops. All *unavailable*. Bar one – Chester.

VASSA (*to* BROWN). Are you all right?

The BISHOP OF CHESTER *strolls the grounds at Lambeth Palace. Tending to flowers and enjoying some pineapple.*

CHESTER. Were religion attended to there can be no doubt that the horrific traffic would cease entirely and we'd see no more slavery. Yet I fear you have too small a voice to be heard.

GRANVILLE. Which is precisely why I have come to you.

BROWN. It's a racket. See, on the slave voyages, captain has *slops* – boots, jackets, supplies – which we have to buy to replace our own.

GRANVILLE. With the Church's help we might bring awareness.

CHESTER. It is unfortunate.

GRANVILLE. It is murder.

BROWN. Well you run up so high a bill by the time you come home you've spent all your wages before you've got 'em, in fact you owe the company now. So what then? Straight back out on the next ship running. Smart fucking racket I tell ya.

VASSA. More of you could speak out.

BROWN. To who?

CHESTER. But are you sure?

GRANVILLE. What?

BROWN. It's the slavers or the wars.

CHESTER. Slaves are prone to revolt.

BROWN. Captain bullies the men, men torture the slaves, slaves' hearts break with despair.

GRANVILLE. Are you a man of God or aren't you?

CHESTER. I beg your pardon?

VASSA. If you rallied together –

GRANVILLE. Do you believe the idea of slavery irreligious?

CHESTER. Complicated.

GRANVILLE. Simple.

VASSA. It is information about *The Zong* I'm after.

CHESTER. The Bible both condemns and condones –

GRANVILLE. Therefore the Church may pick and choose its moral position dependent on its own interests?

CHESTER. You should go.

BROWN (*sings*). *Oh Tommy's gone, what shall I do?*

GRANVILLE. There is a plantation in Barbados, Codrington – I assisted a runaway – the Church of England has a stake in that very plantation, does it not?

CHESTER. Negroes are not Christian. They are heathen. Without the Church they cannot be saved.

GRANVILLE. And without them you cannot subsist.

BROWN. Knew the carpenter on that ship. Captain didn't know his arse from his elbow. He said.

GRANVILLE. If you will not condemn slavery you certainly cannot condone murder. Murder has been committed. What do you intend to do about it?

VASSA. Names.

BROWN. No chance. I didn't want no part of it.

VASSA. Of what...? You were on *The Zong*?

BROWN. What's it to you?

GRANVILLE. What do you intend to do about it?

BROWN. What you gonna do about it? My brother-in-law works down the ironworks, making the chains for them slavers, all his life.

CHESTER. You father was archdeacon, was he not?

BROWN. He don't know nothing about what goes on out on them ships.

GRANVILLE. Northumberland.

BROWN. And I wouldn't tell him.

CHESTER. Then you of all people should appreciate the tremendous power of prayer.

GRANVILLE. Prayer?!

BROWN. He's got kids to feed.

CHESTER. Prayer. Sir, I am not the cause of this brutality.

GRANVILLE. Neither are you actively the cure. Therefore you are the cause.

CHESTER. How dare you?

BROWN. The only ones who can know what them niggers really go through is us and the only ones who can truly comprehend what we go through is them.

VASSA *turns*.

GRANVILLE. What I appreciate is that inaction is a form of brutality. (*Turns*.)

CHESTER. You never followed your father to the Church. Hmm. Inaction. (*Disappears*.)

BROWN. Mate...? (*Holds out his hand*.) I've not eaten these three days...

VASSA *holds out a coin for him but snatches it away before* BROWN *can take it –*

VASSA. I believe you were on *The Zong* and I believe you know something. If you do, now is the chance to do something about this smart bloody racket. Tell me what you know.

BROWN. First mate. Kelsall. He's the one you want. Democratic demon.

VASSA. Who?

A DOCK OFFICER *approaches them –*

DOCK OFFICER. You there!

BROWN. Oh shit the bed, here we go.

DOCK OFFICER (*arriving*). What are you doing there?

BROWN. Nothing, officer.

DOCK OFFICER. Not you. (*To* VASSA.) You.

VASSA. I... –

BROWN (*to the* DOCK OFFICER). An old seamate of mine. Good lad, this.

DOCK OFFICER. What's his name then?

BROWN. Errrm... Black... Man. Thomas Blackman.

DOCK OFFICER. Go.

BROWN *and* VASSA *both turn to go*.

Not you.

VASSA *turns back as* BROWN *runs –*

What is your name?

VASSA. Gustavus Vassa.

DOCK OFFICER. The truth.

VASSA. It is the truth. Gustavus Vassa.

DOCK OFFICER. Why did he lie?

VASSA. I don't know.

DOCK OFFICER (*correcting him*). Sir.

VASSA. Sir.

DOCK OFFICER. Why were you talking to him?

VASSA. He was talking to me.

DOCK OFFICER. Don't get smart. What about?

VASSA. Nothing, sir… his travels. I haven't done anything wrong, sir.

DOCK OFFICER. Like what?

VASSA. Like nothing. We were…

DOCK OFFICER. You paid him money.

VASSA. I didn't pay him, I gave it. He said he was hungry.

DOCK OFFICER. And what did you say to him?

VASSA. I gave him a coin. Sir, you might have asked him?

DOCK OFFICER. I'm asking you.

VASSA. I –

DOCK OFFICER. Step over here.

VASSA. I haven't done anything.

DOCK OFFICER. Here.

He searches VASSA *roughly.*

VASSA. You're hurting me.

DOCK OFFICER. Increase in cargo thefts on these docks of late. The government will have it stopped. Oh yes. (*Re: VASSA's shirt.*) Fine shirt this. Where'd you get it?

VASSA. I bought it.

He flinches and the DOCK OFFICER *lunges at him and wrestles him to the ground.*

You're hurting me –

DOCK OFFICER. Bought it with what?

VASSA (*erupts*). My own wages. My name is Gustavus Vassa of Westman Lane, Lambeth. I am a barber. I cut gentlemen's hair. And I bought these clothes with my own money.

AMA. Help me. Don't leave me.

VASSA (*to the* DOCK OFFICER). Get off me. You're going to take me. Get off me!

DOCK OFFICER. Calm yourself –

AMA. Don't leave me. Rise up!

The DOCK OFFICER *and* VASSA *struggle.*

VASSA. You're going to take me. You're stealing me. Leave us alone! Leave her alone! Help! Father!! Help us. Leave her alone!!

The DOCK OFFICER *is shocked at* VASSA*'s meltdown. He tries to calm* VASSA, *recognising trauma.*

DOCK OFFICER. Calm, calm yourself.

VASSA. Get away from me. You're going to take her!

DOCK OFFICER. There's no one here. Steady. Steady.

VASSA *is shaking but calms down. Each afraid of the other.*

You people. (*Letting go.*) Go on. Go home. You don't belong here.

VASSA *pulls away and runs.*

Scene Three

GRANVILLE*'s house*.

GRANVILLE. Bastards! I'll bring the whole thing down.

VASSA. I'm coming with you.

GRANVILLE (*noticing* VASSA). What happened?

VASSA. Bastards.

GRANVILLE (*uneasy*). You're all right?

VASSA. I have a name. Kelsall. First mate. In London
apparently. Couldn't find him.

GRANVILLE. I will. I'll march them all to the gallows myself.

VASSA. What did you find?

GRANVILLE. The owner of *The Zong* – this William Gregson,
was mayor in Liverpool. His son-in-law, who owns the ship
with him, is mayor currently. The city is drenched in it. They
all know it's wrong. The bishop. The admiralty, they all
reacted in the same way. They looked at me as if I were...

VASSA. Black?

GRANVILLE. What I mean is, this thing has a power.

VASSA. The paper said 'The narrative seemed to make every
person in the court shudder.'

GRANVILLE. Well – who wouldn't shudder that heard this?

Beat.

VASSA. You could be right.

GRANVILLE. What? What are you saying?

VASSA. You said it. Who wouldn't shudder that heard this?
What if you took it and made the whole of Britain shudder?

Beat.

GRANVILLE. Slavery would be done. As would the sugar, the
cotton, the rum. Do you think I have not tried?

VASSA. With this?

AMA (*to* VASSA). Keep going.

VASSA. These people need help.

GRANVILLE. We don't even know precisely who's guilty –

AMA (*to* VASSA). Don't stop.

VASSA (*to* GRANVILLE). Well. You are Judge Mansfield. Who would you say is guilty?

GRANVILLE. The captain of course. Whoever was in command when the deed was done.

VASSA. And the crew who carried out the deed?

GRANVILLE. Them too.

AMA (*to* VASSA). Come on.

VASSA. And the ship's owners who mean to profit by the deed? The insurers who underwrite such deeds?

GRANVILLE (*catching up with him*). The court that justifies such deeds.

VASSA (*catching up with his own thought*). The king who builds his cities and empire on them.

GRANVILLE. Anyone who lifts a spoon of sugar to sweeten their tea.

VASSA. Yes.

AMA. Yes!

GRANVILLE. Yes. The empire is fat with slavery. Mansfield must protect it. This is the problem. (*Reading from the paper.*) 'The jury… *without going out of court* found in favour of the traders…' As quickly and quietly as possible that no one need know. They want this kept from the public.

VASSA. So you give it to the public.

GRANVILLE. But they won't hear the evidence.

VASSA. Will the evidence not be heard in court? If you document the hearing. Transcription. How fast can you write?

GRANVILLE. I might know someone. A shorthand writer. The best.

VASSA. Who?

GRANVILLE. William Woodfall.

VASSA. The actor?

GRANVILLE. Former actor. Owns the paper that published that letter.

VASSA. Good. Where is he?

GRANVILLE. Prison. Well, he was. The Tories didn't like what he was publishing. He's out now. I think. I'm due in Fleet Street. Come. (*He moves off.*)

VASSA. Can't. I'm late. There's a memorial at Gray's Inn. For Ignatius Sancho.

GRANVILLE. Sancho? He was a fine man.

VASSA. Ottobah Cugoano is speaking. I could ask him – ?

GRANVILLE. Cugoano? Unwise.

VASSA. You disapprove of him?

GRANVILLE. His methods.

VASSA. He and some of the other Blacks are starting a newspaper with the help of the Quakers. Could be useful.

GRANVILLE. A newspaper? For who?

VASSA. The Blacks of London. And 'whom' I believe is the correct grammar.

Music. OTTOBAH CUGOANO *is addressing a large crowd of Black Londoners and Quakers at a memorial gathering in a Gray's Inn backroom.*

OTTOBAH. Friends! God is laughing now. Who could not when Ignatius Sancho is in their company? The Coal Black Jolly African. Fat Sancho. Who, if he could have married rum – would have. Great in heart, in form, and mind. I have seen him see off a platter of pickled mackerel and a pot of burgundy in two minutes flat and seen him chase an urchin across the square for shouting out that he looked like nothing so much as a Christmas pudding with legs. We miss him.

Agreement in the room.

One time in Soho he and I passed one of these young fashionables, who laughed to his mate – 'Smoke Othello!' Sancho drew up and exclaimed – 'Aye, sir, such Othellos you meet with but once a century. Such Iagos as you, we meet with in every dirty passage. Proceed!'

Laughter. VASSA *enters and stands at the back.*

He belonged only to God and himself.

PERSON. Sancho the Great!

OTTOBAH. His birthday just gone saw the party rage till it was only he and I left and he began to speak, in the wee hours, of the wonders of life. Of philosophy, religion, art, the wines he had tasted. Of women and the nature of friendship. Dawn and not a sound in all London save Sancho, as he came to his grand theme – Africa. Though he had never seen it – for they say he was born on the slave ship –

PERSON. Truth.

OTTOBAH. Yet he knew Africa. Enlightened *me*, Africa-born.

He knew how to spin muslin. Knew of yams, plantains, eadas and Indian corn.

PERSON. You're making me hungry!

OTTOBAH. And though he had no use of African languages, he could dance. Understood the mysteries of movement. That hips whisper and buttocks shout. He wished that he could have been in Africa just once –

PERSON. He's there now!

OTTOBAH. I said – your blood was boiled in Africa, Ignatius. Bones carved of rare roots.

Agreement.

He taught us. Now we must teach ourselves. Slavery is sin.

QUAKER. Amen.

QUAKER. And we stand with you.

OTTOBAH. For so sayeth the law of God: 'He that stealeth a man and make merchandise of him, that thief shall die.'

PERSON. Brother Cugoano, amen, but I beg not tonight. Can we not just celebrate our brother –

PERSON. Shhh –

OTTOBAH. No, no. Speak.

PERSON. Must you always throw slavery at us?

PERSON. Are you mad?

PERSON. I know, I know, but none of us here are slaves. What's the point of being free if we're still chained to slavery?

OTTOBAH. True. True. I know you are hungry. Let's eat. As Sancho would want. But tell me this, what will you eat with? Hand me that fork.

Someone does.

See this? It's made by a man who not only owns factories in Sheffield but who also owns human factories in Jamaica. And what's more you'd better eat standing up because what does it say on those barrels? Colston. Bristol man, who, if a dozen of us in here were not taken on one of his ships, I'll eat my hat. So go ahead and eat your bellies full and celebrate but whether you like it or not you are sitting in it. This little fork and the building it's in are statues to slavery and in a hundred years' time they'll be treasures for someone to marvel at, when you are long gone. But I know one thing, people will be talking about Ignatious Sancho loooong after slavery is done. I don't ask you to be defined by slavery, I dare you to outlive it!

Agreement. VASSA *tries to catch* OTTOBAH*'s attention.*

This is the work we are called to. We are a community now. I know you are angry. But we must focus that anger. Get furious but get shit done. Organise. We need education. A paper. I shared my dream with Sancho that night. He nodded. 'For thou shalt know the truth, and the truth shall set you free.' Well, you are free now Sancho. Shining in the cradle of ages. Till we meet again, brother.

They toast Sancho. As OTTOBAH *moves from the podium, through the crowd and out of the building,* VASSA *follows him.*

VASSA. Ottobah, I must speak with you –

OTTOBAH. You missed the start. You've been seen with a new lady recently.

VASSA. I have something to tell you.

OTTOBAH. Not Black, this lady. They say. Miss Susannah Cullen? Is it true?

VASSA. Oto, this is serious.

OTTOBAH. Where were you? I thought something had happened.

VASSA. Something has happened.

OTTOBAH. What?

VASSA. Killings. On a slave ship. Hundreds thrown into the sea by the captain in order that he might claim insurance on them. We are trying to find out what happened –

OTTOBAH. *The Zong.*

VASSA. How do you know?

OTTOBAH. Brother Mandeville read about it. Who's 'we'?

VASSA. Me.

OTTOBAH. And?

VASSA. Granville Sharp.

OTTOBAH. Sharp?

VASSA. Yes. It could be something for the paper. He said we should let you know.

OTTOBAH. And you have. I will be sure to thank him at Westminster Hall.

VASSA. You're going?

OTTOBAH. Some of us.

VASSA. You didn't tell me.

OTTOBAH. You weren't here. Remember?

COMPANY (*to us*). At that very same moment, Granville is trying to meet –

COMPANY. An old ally at his newspaper print house in Fleet Street.

Scene Four

WOODFALL*'s print house, Fleet Street.*

GRANVILLE *is trying to keep up with* WOODFALL *as he moves around his chaotic print room, inspecting the printing presses being manned by his busy* WORKERS.

GRANVILLE. William, you published the letter, how can you not know who sent it?

WOODFALL. They didn't sign it. Not a taxing concept.

GRANVILLE. Still you published it.

WOODFALL. This may shock you but you no longer have the monopoly on slavery hatred, my dear.

GRANVILLE. Then you'll come?

WOODFALL. I'm busy.

GRANVILLE. Slavery will end, William.

WOODFALL. But you or I shall not see it.

He tightens one of the press screws one of the workers is struggling with.

Oh no no nooo! This is no good. Do it again please.

GRANVILLE. We need a shorthand writer. You're the best. William, someone wrote that letter. I offer you a follow-up.

WOODFALL. Oh, you're helping *me*?

GRANVILLE. The owner, Gregson? And the insurer, Gilbert, what do you know of them? We know the first mate, Kelsall, is in London. Help me find him.

WOODFALL. The British public are not interested in insurance losses, Granville, they are interested in the loss of America and their fifty thousand dead sons. They are more interested in the Prince of Wales farting at passers by in St James's Park than they are a few drowned Blacks a thousand miles away.

He corrects the BOY *loading the press.*

GRANVILLE. 'We hold these truths to be self-evident' –

WOODFALL. 'All men created equal. Life, liberty', yes, yes, yes.

GRANVILLE. Equal. Washington has won the war with it.

WOODFALL. And it'll be the end of the prime minister, mark my words. (*To the* BOY, *dissatisfied with the page he's been handed*.) I cannot read this. Keep the press down *longer*. Again please. (*To* GRANVILLE.) They'll ruin me.

GRANVILLE. *All* men equal. Now slavery must go.

WOODFALL. But not just yet, my dear. For the same reason Mansfield has never allowed you any true victory in this irksome matter and will not let you win now – *profit*. Britain has just lost one of her most valued possessions, she will not give up the other. (*To the* BOY.) Jesus wept. Again! (*To* GRANVILLE.) Equal?! Your man Franklin drafted that declaration with one hand while wielding a whip over a plantation full of slaves with the other.

GRANVILLE. You do not pity Blacks?

WOODFALL. Slavery is not about race, it is about greed.

GRANVILLE. Which you oppose.

WOODFALL. And lost twelve months for, at the hands of Mansfield! And almost lost this paper.

GRANVILLE. So...?

WOODFALL. Stay home.

GRANVILLE. Not possible. Come with us.

WOODFALL. Not possible.

GRANVILLE. Come with us.

WOODFALL. And will you come with me to the gallows after I do?

GRANVILLE. They'll not –

WOODFALL. Not *you*, no. Because you are a punter, a groundling. You will sit in Westminster Hall and squint and tut. If I go into that court we'll simply make it easier for them. When my father ran this paper, if you spoke out against the government, you were a housefly to be batted away – speak out today and you are the disease. To be wiped out. Cleansed from the body politic.

GRANVILLE. Why did you print that letter?

A scream. The BOY *has his hand caught in the press.* WOODFALL *grabs him.*

(*To* GRANVILLE.) Move that! Dear God.

Finally they wrench the screaming BOY*'s bloody hand from the hinge. Another* WORKER *takes him off. When they are alone –*

WOODFALL. You should not have come. Listen to me –

GRANVILLE. No, you listen, there were those in America who said 'We will never be independent of the British. Stay home.' And now look. I have never been holed up on a slave ship, but I can imagine. And there are thousands in this country who will do the same, and when they do slavery will be done once and for all. But first they must be told. You will write of *The Zong*, Bill. For if you do not write about this, then never write more.

WOODFALL. How much will your average Black fetch these days?

GRANVILLE. Forty pounds. Same as that printer.

WOODFALL. That is the latest model. Cost me fifty.

GRANVILLE *is not amused.*

I printed that letter because words matter. And the word
you're talking about is Rights. Everyone bandies it now.
Rights for the Americans. For French peasants. Ladies.

GRANVILLE. Blacks. Humans.

WOODFALL. Take that word into Mansfield's court and they'll
eat us alive. These people are not fucking around.

GRANVILLE. If the Church is deaf and the Law is blind then
the papers are all we have.

Silence.

William...?

WOODFALL. Once more unto the breach, dear friend. I hope
you know what you're doing.

GRANVILLE. Bring plenty of ink.

Scene Five

The hold of The Zong.

AMA *is muttering in the darkness of the cramped hold.*

RIBA. Who are you talking to?

AMA. Him.

RIBA. Who?

AMA. Someone is trying to help me. They're coming.

RIBA. Who?

AMA. Don't know. A man of feeling. I must tell him how to
reach –

RIBA. There's no one here –

AMA. At least he's trying. What are you doing? We've been
here too long.

RIBA. Just wait –

AMA. You speak the white man's language. Find out what they intend. All you say is wait. I'm done with you. (*Turns her back on the* WOMEN.)

RIBA. Ama?!

JOYI *cries out from a nightmare*. RIBA *calms her*.

Shhh, Joyi. Still bad dreams?

JOYI. My mother's face. I was thinking of my mother but I couldn't see her face. I couldn't remember her face, Riba!

RIBA. Calm.

JOYI. What if the tree was true? What if we do forget?

RIBA. No, shh.

JOYI. What if this baby is pink like them? Like *him*. I do not think I can survive this.

RIBA. What's the first thing you will do when we get home?

JOYI. Sleep. You?

RIBA. Pray

JOYI. Why?

RIBA. That my mother doesn't beat me too bad for being gone so long.

JOYI. Ha. Yes.

RIBA. Ama?

AMA. Leave me alone.

RIBA. What does your mother look like, Joyi?

JOYI. Tall –

RIBA. Mine too –

JOYI. With those little freckles our mothers get on their cheeks –

RIBA. Yes. What will she be doing?

JOYI. Cooking. (*Smiles.*) Singing. Everything she would do, she would sing. Plaiting our hair, washing, digging. She'd never beat us –

RIBA. Didn't need to. Just give you that look –

JOYI. And you knew –

RIBA. Ha ha. Yes. You see? What about yours, Ama?

JOYI. She wants to be left alone.

RIBA. Alone is not good. (*So that* AMA *can hear.*) She is ashamed. But she'll learn. She's no good to us dead.

JOYI. She looks like she can't remember her mother either. What if it happens again, Riba?

RIBA. What will your mother be cooking, Joyi? What's your favourite?

Beat.

JOYI. Jollof rice –

RIBA. How will she cook it?

JOYI. She gets that large pot. Fries up the pepper and onions –

RIBA. Mine would start with the beef. Season the beef, then add –

JOYI. That's not how you make jollof –

RIBA. Yes, Joyi. Season the beef –

JOYI. You asked me about *my* mother. I don't know what *your* mother was cooking –

RIBA. Jollof.

JOYI. Not proper jollof –

RIBA. Yes, Joyi –

AMA. Water. She heats the water in her large pot with sliced onion and pepper. Then she adds the seasoned meat. Lets me put the cover on it and lets it cook till the smells begin to drift up and the meat starts to tender. 'No salt yet or it won't cook.' She cuts up tomatoes and garlic, adds some oil, mixes it all and lets it cook till it's brown and you can't resist.

'Remember to keep stirring though. Don't let it burn.'
Finally she pours in the rice. Always adds an extra handful –
'For the walkers', as Grandmother used to say. Lets me
cover the pot, lets it cook and cook and somehow by the time
everyone is home it is ready to eat.

JOYI. That's the way –

RIBA. We are the *walkers* now. They will be ready for us when
we return.

AMA. It's those times I miss most.

JOYI. Me too. (*To* RIBA.) What do you miss most?

RIBA. My children.

AMA. Before we eat we always give thanks to God. But where
is God now? Why does he allow this to happen to us?

*The ship suddenly lurches, shudders and rocks. A deep
churning sound. The* WOMEN *are knocked off-balance.*

RIBA. Shhh!!

JOYI. What?

AMA. What is it?!

JOYI. What's happening? Riba?!

RIBA. We are turning round –

JOYI. What's happening?

RIBA. We are turning round. Feel.

JOYI. The boat is turning.

AMA. What does this mean?

RIBA. It means we are facing home.

RIBA, *with quiet determination, hums 'The Song of
Unforgetting' as the ship sways. The* WOMEN *join her.*

Scene Six

Outside GRANVILLE's *house*.

COMPANY (*to us*). Sunday evening. The night before the hearing –

COMPANY. Granville and Gustav are surprised by a stranger appearing –

GRANVILLE *and* VASSA *are at* GRANVILLE's *door. A young woman walks up from the shadows*.

ANNIE. Mister Sharp?

GRANVILLE. Yes.

ANNIE. You're late home. I called to your house this afternoon but you were gone. I got soaked.

GRANVILLE. Well?

ANNIE. Mister Woodfall sent me.

GRANVILLE. Why?

ANNIE. He was taken into custody this morning.

GRANVILLE. Why?

ANNIE. He didn't say. He wrote me that you require a secretary. A hearing? Here I am. (*She holds out her papers*.) He said you were not to worry and that I was precisely what you are looking for.

GRANVILLE. Did he? Come in. (*Gestures to* VASSA.) Mister... er...

VASSA. Vassa.

Extends his hand. ANNIE *is unsure*. GRANVILLE *checks out the references*.

GRANVILLE. You would accompany us at court tomorrow morning.

VASSA. A full transcript. Do you –

GRANVILLE. Thank you, Mister Vassa. A full transcript. Two shillings. You have been before at Westminster Hall?

ANNIE. No.

VASSA. It's beside the Abbey.

ANNIE. I know.

GRANVILLE. Name?

ANNIE. Anne.

GRANVILLE. Anne what?

ANNIE. Greenwood. It's on my paper.

GRANVILLE. I know.

ANNIE. You look confused.

GRANVILLE. Which system do you use?

ANNIE. Sorry?

GRANVILLE. Shorthand. Byrom? Shelton...?

ANNIE. Oh, I have my own system. I invented it. Some of those other ways I found too slow. My way I can write faster.

GRANVILLE. I see. Well, Miss, er – . My associate and I have important business –

ANNIE. You suppose I cannot write as I say.

GRANVILLE. Correct. We can have no mistakes. Our purposes require a shorthand writer –

ANNIE. To accompany you at Westminster Hall and make transcripts of everything which is spoken. Which I can do. Excellently. You presume my being a female renders this statement untrue. Which would be a mistake. This is not the sixteenth century.

VASSA. It says here you are at Montagu House at the new British Museum.

ANNIE. Was. The library. You have almost as many books here. Now I teach.

GRANVILLE. Who?

ANNIE. Children. You remember them – little people – eat a lot. I teach them to read. Think.

VASSA *laughs*. ANNIE *turns on him*.

Can you read?

VASSA. Excellently.

ANNIE *takes the* Morning Chronicle *from* GRANVILLE, *hands it to* VASSA.

ANNIE. Read.

ANNIE *takes a quill and writes as* VASSA *reads*.

VASSA. 'I wish some man of feeling would give poetical language to one of those brave African's thoughts. With what noble disdain would he animate his sentiments? What tender adieu would he bid his family and country? What parting look would he cast on a glorious world disgraced by such a scene?'

ANNIE (*reads back*). 'I wish some man of feeling would give poetical language to one of those brave African's thoughts. With what noble disdain would he animate his sentiments? What tender adieu would he bid his family and country? What parting look would he cast on a glorious world disgraced by such a scene?'

GRANVILLE *cuts her off*.

GRANVILLE. Westminster Hall. Tomorrow. Eleven o'clock.

ANNIE. Sharp. (*Goes*.)

VASSA. Do you think Woodfall will be –

GRANVILLE. Read that again.

VASSA. What?

GRANVILLE. That. The rest of *The Zong* letter.

VASSA. 'I wish some man of feeling would give poetical language to one of those brave African's thoughts. With what noble disdain would he animate his sentiments? What tender adieu would he bid his family and country? What parting look would he cast on a glorious world disgraced by such a scene?'

GRANVILLE. Whoever wrote this letter instructs us.

VASSA. How?

GRANVILLE. *I wish some man of feeling.* Empathy.

VASSA. Empathy?

GRANVILLE. From the Greek, meaning feeling. *I wish some man of feeling would give language to their thoughts.* The writer challenges us, dares us to see these as human beings. Not a slave but a *human being* who happens to be *enslaved.* A person with thoughts and feelings. Reason. Desires. Passions. You are ahead of me in that regard.

VASSA. Me?

GRANVILLE. I've never been on one, you have.

VASSA. I wasn't on *The Zong.*

GRANVILLE. A slave ship I mean. (*Beat.*) How else did you get here?

VASSA. Britain? An English captain. During the Seven Years' War. I told you. Pascal. I fought under him. It was he who christened me Vassa. Said I looked like the King of Sweden –

GRANVILLE. No, I mean prior to that. Before the war.

VASSA. Before?

GRANVILLE. Yes. Where were you originally from? (*Beat.*) Africa...

AMA (*to* VASSA). Answer him –

VASSA (*stares*). I... Don't...?

GRANVILLE. How did this Pascal... – I mean... you must have... Where were you born?

AMA. Answer him.

VASSA *thinks and slowly raises his arm, pointing in a distant direction... reconsiders then slowly points, even more unsure, in the opposite direction. His arm slowly falls to his side.*

GRANVILLE. What were you called before he named you for a Swedish king?

VASSA....Michael.

Beat.

GRANVILLE. And before that?

VASSA....Thomas.

GRANVILLE....And before that?

VASSA....Jacob...

GRANVILLE....And before...

AMA. No name. No home. No Africa. Nothing.

GRANVILLE *shifts and stares at* VASSA. *A realisation makes him very uneasy.*

GRANVILLE (*censoring himself*). The war certainly must have been... difficult... disturbing for one so young.

VASSA. Captain Pascal taught me to read.

GRANVILLE. I lost my father when I was young.

VASSA. I don't want to talk about those things.

GRANVILLE. I think you are *a brave man of feeling*, Mister... Vassa... (*Pause.*) Did this Pascal teach you to how pray?

VASSA. Yes.

GRANVILLE. Come.

They kneel and pray. 'The Song of Unforgetting' is heard underneath. A church version. The music and the image of VASSA *and* GRANVILLE *hold as we transition to next morning. The court of Westminster Hall is created by the company in front of us.*

BOTH. Our Father which art in heaven,
   Hallowed be thy name.
   Thy kingdom come,
   Thy will be done in earth,
   As it is in heaven.
   Give us this day our daily bread.
   And forgive us our trespasses,
   As we forgive those...
   Who trespass against us –

Scene Seven

Westminster Hall.

COMPANY *(to us)*. Stand in Parliament Square facing Big Ben and the building directly in front of you is Westminster Hall.

COMPANY. The trials of Guy Fawkes –

COMPANY. Thomas More –

COMPANY. And William Wallace all in this room.

VASSA. But on –

ANNIE *(writing)*. May 21st, in the year of Our Lord, 1783.

COMPANY *(to us)*. Though some tried to erase it from the bookshelves of history, what you are about to hear actually happened.

ANNIE. We wrote it down. The transcript is in Greenwich Maritime Museum today.

COMPANY. The trial –

COMPANY. Not a trial! An appeal to decide whether the extraordinary case of *The Zong* should be reheard.

OTTOBAH *(taking his seat)*. Gustav.

VASSA. Are the others with you?

OTTOBAH *gestures behind him to us – the audience*.

COURT CLERK. His Majesty's King's Court Bench is now in session. All rise for the Lord Chief Justice Mansfield.

MANSFIELD. Right. Let's get on with it. (*Reads the declaration*.)

'Gregson vs Gilbert. Motion for retrial. A case of a policy of insurance upon the slave ship *The Zong*. Belonging to plaintiff, Mister William Gregson and Co. of Liverpool, to recover the value of one hundred and thirty-two slaves thrown overboard and drowned of necessity on account of perils of the sea and want of water. They were forced, as the captain said, to throw several of the Negroes overboard. In short there was an absolute Necessity for doing so and the great Misfortune arose from mistaking Jamaica for Hispaniola which carried them out of their Course. The Question was, whether there was an Absolute Necessity for throwing the Negroes overboard. The jury were of the opinion there was and found for the plaintiffs. The Negroes being valued thirty pounds per head, the sum requested of the underwriters for lost chattels amounts three thousand, nine hundred and sixty pounds.'

COMPANY (*to us*). For the Liverpool ship owners, the newly appointed Attorney General of England, Sir John Lee. Known around Westminster as 'Honest Jack'.

LEE. My lord, this is a case of chattels and goods. British law is clear: Blacks are property. This property was thrown overboard of necessity to save the vessel.

COMPANY (*to us*). And for the insurers, Arthur Leary Pigott. Not at the first trial. Which his side lost. Young blood brought in to overturn the verdict.

PIGOTT. My lord, I am astonished how this verdict was originally obtained. When looked into it cannot stand.

OTTOBAH (*to us*). Oh FYI, Pigott's father: one of the biggest slave owners in the Caribbean. So, plaintiffs – slave owners; insurers – slave traders; lawyers – slave owners.

MANSFIELD. *Let justice be done though the heavens fall*.

GRANVILLE (*to us*). Judge – slave owner. It was a convention.

MANSFIELD. Mister Pigott, upon what ground do you appeal a new trial be heard?

PIGOTT. That perils of the sea, as stated in their declaration, was *not* in fact the cause of the ship's slow voyage. The captain's own negligence was. And that their witness Robert Stubbs swore to a necessity that did not exist.

MANSFIELD. We heard no evidence but his. There was no other witness alive.

LEE. Stubbs was on *The Zong* a passenger and therefore the only person that could be said to be perfectly disinterested in this question.

OLAUDAH (*to us*). Stubbs that very moment was not in Westminster Hall, but at the Old Bailey in that corruption dispute with his former employer mentioned at the start of the play.

MANSFIELD (*checking notes*). Stubbs swore he was bred to the sea –

STUBBS (*pops up*). *I was bred to the sea.*

MANSFIELD. – that he was on the West Coast of Africa –

STUBBS. Appointed Governor at Annamaboe slave port in 1781.

MANSFIELD. – took passage aboard *The Zong*.

STUBBS. Left Africa August 18th. Took a hundred blessed days to crawl cross the Atlantic. Everyone sick, including Captain Collingwood. He fires First Mate Kelsall and begs me to take charge, which – since I've commanded ships in the past – I do. Finally – they sight the West Indies; Hispaniola, which your lordships will doubtless know is held by the blasted French. So they sail on three days – only to realise that which they'd avoided was in fact the island of our destination.

MANSFIELD. Jamaica?

STUBBS. Easy enough mistake. Them islands – all look the same to me. So, back we go. Only now with the winds it's eleven days return instead of three. Then they discover the water butts have leaked. So, November 29th, they begin chucking the sickest Blacks into the sea. We'd have died otherwise.

PIGOTT. My lord, Stubbs stated there were three butts of water remaining on the 29th. They could have given every person on board two quarts a day. *Anticipated* necessity perhaps – not *absolute necessity*. Furthermore, this *The Zong* was a four-mast ship at two hundred tonnes. Carrying four hundred and forty-two chattels. Um… It is calculated a ship of this size would house no more than three hundred. *The Zong* was a recklessly overcrowded ship before she had even left Africa.

MANSFIELD. What is the meaning of *Zong*?

PIGOTT. I don't… know, my lord. (*Leans in to* MANSFIELD *slightly. Off-record.*) My anxiety is, my lord, knowing the extent of the trade and the immense consequence it is for Britain –

MANSFIELD (*cutting him off*). That is out of the cause, Mister Pigott.

PIGOTT (*more carefully*). My lord, for the sake of the trade, I wish that it might never come to question in point of law –

MANSFIELD (*pointedly*). You talk out of the cause!

PIGOTT. In. It never was from the beginning of the trade till this moment that the underwriters were ever called upon to pay the loss arising from the Mortality of Slaves –

MANSFIELD. Mister Pigott –

PIGOTT. And whatever the cause it would be of so great an inconvenience to the trade if the underwriters were made liable.

MANSFIELD. It is not in the cause. Move on.

VASSA. What's he saying?

OTTOBAH. Defending the trade. Whitewash.

GRANVILLE (*to* ANNIE). Why have you stopped?

    ANNIE *reluctantly continues to write.*

VASSA (*to* OTTOBAH). The ship was smaller than that.

OTTOBAH. What?

VASSA. He doesn't know what he's talking about. It was three masts, not four.

OTTOBAH. Say.

GRANVILLE. Gentlemen.

OTTOBAH (*to* VASSA). Tell them!

GRANVILLE. Gentlemen!

MANSFIELD (*from the court*). The Negroes at the back will kindly control themselves.

OTTOBAH (*publicly*). The ship was smaller than that!

PIGOTT. My point is the ship was too small to carry so many. This incompetent captain's overcrowding of the ship is what led to the crisis.

LEE. My learned friend's clients, the underwriters, were more than happy to insure the entire number of slaves regardless whether the ship was the size of a canoe or the Ark.

MANSFIELD. Gentlemen.

PIGOTT. Of course the ship's logbook could tell us precisely the numbers on board, state of the water supplies and who made the navigational errors.

MANSFIELD. Where is it?

LEE. Missing, my lord.

MANSFIELD. Missing? Could nothing on this ship be kept on board?

PIGOTT. I did request it of the owners. Nothing. Were that log to be present, these proceedings would be deciding a case of fraud. To avoid such, I assume the book was destroyed by the owners. The court's verdict must therefore be overturned.

MANSFIELD. The question is, was it an act of absolute necessity?

PIGOTT. No. And I am hardly surprised that neither the owners, captain, nor mariners are here. I venture to predict they never will be seen –

LEE. The poor captain, Collingwood, died seven days after they finally reached Jamaica.

PIGOTT. Instead a passenger, this Stubbs, is fetched up to explain the whole transaction –

LEE. And gave his evidence with as much sympathy and tenderness as ever I saw in my life.

MANSFIELD. I understand it is the law that if slaves die a natural death at sea the underwriters do not pay. *But* if the slaves attack the crew and are killed, they shall be paid for as damages done to goods?

LEE. Correct.

MANSFIELD. Just as if horses had been thrown overboard.

LEE. Maritime law is quite clear. Any vessel finding itself at the mercy of perils of the sea – storms, et cetera, has by law the right to jettison cargo – barrels, chests, chattel – to save the vessel. These Negroes were bought and paid for under the law as cargo.

ANNIE. Mister Sharp??

GRANVILLE. Shhh!

OTTOBAH (*to* VASSA). Are you hearing this?

LEE. The insurer takes upon him the risk of the loss of slaves.

VASSA....Loss.

PIGOTT. There was no loss in the usual sense. These chattels were deliberately thrown into the sea.

LEE. And? Stubbs swore if one hundred did not die in this way, two hundred should in another –

PIGOTT. Precisely. Dead slaves fetch no profit. The truth is this fraud was carried out to saddle a bad market upon my clients.

LEE. Fraud? Stubbs swore not one of the crew knew anything of insurance.

MANSFIELD. But as administrator at the slave port he might?

OTTOBAH. Yes!

MANSFIELD. Who was that?

VASSA. Oto.

OTTOBAH. Devils!

ANNIE. Mister Sharp?

LEE. Any British master owning Blacks has by law an unquestionable right to throw overboard as many as he pleases.

PIGOTT. But he does not have the right to commit fraud!

MANSFIELD. Gentlemen!

LEE. Sir, if a trader cannot insure his own property then how would there be any trade?!

GRANVILLE. There!!

The implications flash through the courtroom. Westminster Hall has a pre-SHUDDER.

MANSFIELD. The matter is – was it necessity? For we have no doubt the case of slaves is the same as if horses had been thrown overboard.

OTTOBAH (*exploding*). Then use horses!

Uproar.

MANSFIELD. What?!

OTTOBAH. This is an offence against God!

MANSFIELD. Order!

VASSA. Oto –

MANSFIELD. Who was that?!

LEE (*looking directly at* GRANVILLE). My lord, I understand there is a person at court who intends to bring a criminal prosecution for murder against the parties concerned –

OTTOBAH. Murderers! According to this court, the taking away of Black lives is of no more account than taking away the life of a beast!

VASSA. Oto!

GRANVILLE. Gentlemen –

MANSFIELD. This is a court of law, not the bush –

OTTOBAH. Then where is justice?

MANSFIELD. Heed me!

LEE. Criminal charges!

OTTOBAH. End the merchandising of men –

VASSA. Oto, no –

OTTOBAH. Are you mad?!

LEE. Ridiculous!

GRANVILLE. Vassa?!

OTTOBAH. End slavery! This is sick. Any man here who does
    not do his Christian duty in the face of this massacre, let him be
    damned and cursed to bloody hell! Vassa, SAY SOMETHING!

MANSFIELD. Out!

OTTOBAH (*as he's dragged out*). And do you yourself not
    have a Negro daughter, Justice Mansfield? What if she had
    been on *The Zong*? Then none of you shall know peace until
    there is justice. (*As he's pushed through the doors*.) None of
    you shall know Peace until there is Justice!!

Doors close. Silence.

MANSFIELD. Do not presume my patience will be tried in this
    place! I am Lord Chief Justice twenty year. This will not
    stand. This is an insurance appeal, no more. Let it carry till
    tomorrow. But let it be understood by all, this court will not
    suffer such conduct then, nor be shook from its purpose. This
    case will be tried under the law and the law is that slaves are
    as horses. (*Gets up*.) Clear this place.

COURT CLERK. All rise!

Scene Eight

Parliament Square.

COMPANY (*to us*). Outside Westminster Hall is now the scene.
Neither Ottobah nor Justice – anywhere to be seen –

GRANVILLE. It's over. If they let us back in tomorrow it will
be a miracle. Thanks to you. I warned against Cugoano.
Where's the girl?

VASSA. How did they know you intend to bring murder
charges? You spoke to Lee. Behind my back?

GRANVILLE. Please. Sir, I've been monitored since my first
Negro trial eighteen years ago. I warned you –

PIGOTT *bumps into* VASSA.

PIGOTT. Watch it!

GRANVILLE. Arthur Pigott! Do more. Stubbs is as guilty as
this First Mate Kelsall. Why did you not bring them?

PIGOTT. Attacking Mansfield will not help your cause –

VASSA. What is your cause?

PIGOTT. Success for my client.

GRANVILLE. The underwriters of human slavery? Themselves
traders? You?

PIGOTT. Not your business. If you cared so much for Negroes
you would have come to that man's aid when he was being
dragged out. We've all heard of your fussing over the Blacks,
Sharp. Is it they who benefit from your bleating on, sir, or
yourself?

GRANVILLE. What?

PIGOTT (*re:* VASSA). At least this one seems to know that
court is less about passion than patience. I should have a care
for your friend, whoever he was.

VASSA. *Care*, Mister Pigott.

PIGOTT. – What?

VASSA. *The Zong*. The ship was built by the Dutch, won by us and sold to a Glasgow trader in Africa before Gregson bought her. Originally called *The Zorgue*, which in the Dutch vernacular translates – *Care*. The English made a mistake on the bill of sale.

PIGOTT. Oh it is a clever one. I know what I am doing. (*Leaves*.)

GRANVILLE. Kelsall is in London. If you knew what you were doing you'd bring him here and hold him to account.

ANNIE *catches up to them*.

ANNIE. Gentlemen. I am sorry, but I will not go back in with you tomorrow.

GRANVILLE. What?

ANNIE. I trust you will accept my apologies.

GRANVILLE. What?

ANNIE. You didn't tell me.

GRANVILLE. Tell you what?

ANNIE. I cannot write down such acts for two shillings, two hundred pounds, nor all the gold in Africa.

GRANVILLE. Is she serious?

ANNIE. How shall I sleep? No, I will not write down your document for you.

GRANVILLE. It is not for me that these atrocities must be made known.

VASSA. Miss Greenwood –

GRANVILLE. You people waste my time.

ANNIE (*to* VASSA). Have you been a slave?

GRANVILLE. Give me the book.

ANNIE (*to* VASSA). Was it as bad as described?

GRANVILLE. The book!

ANNIE. I was told the Africans are better off in America. My brother David was lost there in the battle of Yorktown. He wrote of paradise.

GRANVILLE. Dear God.

VASSA. With respect, was *he* better off in America? Miss Greenwood, I fought in the wars. Poor young Englishmen are afforded only three ways in this country – the prisons or the slavers or the army.

GRANVILLE. Give me the book.

VASSA. Your brother died in the mud. For these same men who own and trade slaves.

GRANVILLE. Give me the book.

ANNIE. But you did not tell me –

GRANVILLE. Tell you what? That human beings do things to one another that beasts would shudder at? You are no different to the rest. You close your eyes to that which is not convenient and say – 'What can I do?' And point your finger at everyone else. Blame everyone else. And the last thing you will ever do is take responsibility for your own bigotry. Gutless.

VASSA. Mister Sharp –

GRANVILLE. Instead, you waltz along to the theatres, the coffee houses and the game rooms when these people at the bottom of the ocean had not the luxury of being able to turn away. Do something. Or fuck off!

VASSA. Stop!

GRANVILLE. Give it me. I will write it myself.

ANNIE (*throwing it on the ground*). If you were a man you would have done so in the first place. You think you are better than the brutes on that ship. You're worse. (*Goes.*)

VASSA. The men on that ship lost themselves. Do not lose yourself, sir.

GRANVILLE. Why, one Desdemona insufficient?

VASSA. What?

GRANVILLE. Taken a liking to this one too?

VASSA. Are you mad? Why do you do this?

GRANVILLE. Because you came to my door in the rain, sir. Or have you forgotten that?

VASSA. Because I was told you were a good man.

GRANVILLE. Because I can get the thing done. Because I will bring slavery down. Because I will not stop until it is dead in the dust. That is why. So do not question me. Question yourself. Whoever you are.

VASSA grabs him by the throat.

Have you lost your mind?!

Suddenly AMA*'s voice is heard: 'The Song of Unforgetting'. For a moment* VASSA *hears and sees her. Comes back to himself, but still enraged and confused.* VASSA *lets go of a shocked* GRANVILLE.

VASSA (*shaking*). No. You do not get to turn me into what you need me to be. (*Disappears into the night.*)

GRANVILLE. Gustav?!

Rain. He is alone.

We see BROWN *come along the dark river. Pissed. He sings as he passes* GRANVILLE, *who walks into the darkness, and tries to make us join him in the song.*

BROWN. *To thee belongs the rural reign,*
Thy cities shall with commerce shine,
All thine shall be the subject main,
And every shore it circles thine.
Rule, Britannia! Britannia rule the waves
Britons never, never, never, shall be slaves.

He is gone.

Scene Nine

Bow Street Gaol. Later that night.

VASSA *has been walking. A* GAOLER *shows him into the cell where* OTTOBAH *is being held.*

GAOLER. 'Tis a quiet night. Keep it that way. Five minutes.

VASSA. Ottobah.

OTTOBAH. You could bring me no food? You must know what I'd love above even the key to this cell is a big piece of chicken.

VASSA. You've not eaten?

OTTOBAH. The only meat here has been freely scuttling back and forth through that hole.

VASSA. I have nothing –

OTTOBAH. Then why have you come?

VASSA. I need to speak with you –

OTTOBAH – Now you have something to say?

VASSA. And you will hear it.

OTTOBAH. I've been here all night.

VASSA. I had to –

OTTOBAH. Drink?

VASSA. – go home.

OTTOBAH. Before or after the alehouse?

VASSA. I have not been to the alehouse.

OTTOBAH (*sniffs.*) Hmm. Where's your friend?

VASSA. Who?... Granville? I have had a – I have – yes, I have, I admit – and if I had, I am perfectly entitled –

OTTOBAH. 'I, I, I' –

VASSA. My concern brought me here.

OTTOBAH. Then forgive me.

VASSA. For?

OTTOBAH. Mistaking feelings of concern for those of guilt.

VASSA. Are you serious?

OTTOBAH. It's not me who is in drink.

VASSA. I'm not – The man in a cell accuses me of guilt.

OTTOBAH. That rat was here sooner than you were.

VASSA. Which one of us is responsible for your being here, Oto?

OTTOBAH. Lower your voice.

VASSA. Answer me.

OTTOBAH. You.

VASSA. I?

OTTOBAH. Yes.

VASSA. No. Are you mad?

OTTOBAH. Disgusted.

VASSA. It was I who drove you to disrupt proceedings? Abuse
    the Lord Chief Justice? You brought you to this state, Oto.
    That demon in you. That rage –

OTTOBAH. And where's yours?

VASSA. Selfish.

OTTOBAH. The tongue wags now. Careful where it leads
    you –

VASSA. You cannot behave so in a court of law and expect to
    see justice.

OTTOBAH. Bollocks.

VASSA. There are people who would kill us –

OTTOBAH. I am prepared to speak and die for my people.

VASSA. You shout over your people.

OTTOBAH. I am here in this hole because I spoke out, because you would not. Damn you. You expect me to sit in silence while those white devils smiled their tale about throwing our sisters to the bottom of the sea?

SHUDDER.

VASSA. Stop.

OTTOBAH. Whilst that judge and those pigs frown and decide not whether it might be a sin but who will suck the profit of it?

VASSA. It's not the way. We are men.

OTTOBAH. Who they fling to the sea in chains and pick up thirty pounds for the trouble. Assault the officer? I care not how many they may be, nor if they wear a sailor's cap, a judge's wig or a crown, the man who thinks he can get away with murdering my people, I will kill him dead. Disrespect the court? These devils have disrespected our people and our land for two hundred years. And you say nothing?

VASSA. You do not know me –

OTTOBAH. I know Gustavus is no African name. I know no African could have sat through that mess and not spoken out.

VASSA. Who are you to stand here and tell me I do not care for Black people?

OTTOBAH. I did not say you did not care for Black people –

VASSA. Push me farther and see how well you know me –

OTTOBAH. Push yourself. You have become passive. And now you call on Dutch courage to liberate your tongue.

VASSA. …Become passive? Since?

OTTOBAH. Yes.

VASSA. Since?

OTTOBAH. I could not have sat there –

VASSA. I have *become…* since…?

OTTOBAH. Your fire should have been in that court –

VASSA. Since I told you of this in the first place? Since I have come here in the dead of night to see about you? Or since I have feelings for a woman who happens to be one of those white devils you talk about? Is *that* what this is about? Susannah Cullen? Because if it is that, Ottobah –

OTTOBAH. It is not the ones who spit on you in the street. It is the ones who wipe their hands after shaking yours.

VASSA. Who are you to tell me –

OTTOBAH. One of your own race. Some brother!

VASSA. What would you have me do? Crawl? Kill? You want me to bleed? (*Taking keys from his pocket.*) I'll do it.

OTTOBAH. Give me those.

VASSA. No, no. You think that I do not feel?

OTTOBAH. Stop!

VASSA (*more cuts*). You think – that I'm a bad brother?

OTTOBAH. Give me those!

VASSA. Why was I not here sooner? Because I was talking to God. Begging forgiveness. Because I am lost here, Ottobah. I am in the storm.

OTTOBAH. Enough.

VASSA. It is never enough. As though somehow because I don't shout and have white acquaintances that I am somehow less Black.

OTTOBAH. Stop.

OTTOBAH *grabs* VASSA, *struggles to take the keys from him –*

VASSA. All the water in that ocean cannot wash the shame off me. Get off me. Get away from me. You're going to take me! Leave her! Leave her alone. Leave her alone!

OTTOBAH. Who?

VASSA. I *am* a bad brother.

OTTOBAH. Listen to me –

VASSA. She could – she could have been on that ship, Oto. My poor sister –

SHUDDER.

OTTOBAH – Your sister?

VASSA. – Supposed to look after her – she, she, –

OTTOBAH. When?

VASSA. He told me. Father... Left our village one morning. Said I was in charge... you the man of the house... look after your sister... look after my house. Then. Two men... a woman – over the walls... they take us... stole us through the forests... hours... trees...

OTTOBAH. Yes –

VASSA. – We cling to each other all night across the man's chest... Next day... NO!... take her... pull her out the door... she would not let go my hand... I tried to hold on but I could not hold her... –

OTTOBAH. Who? What was her name?

VASSA. I can't find her, Oto –

OTTOBAH. What was her name?

VASSA. Promised Father –

OTTOBAH. Who?

VASSA. Rayowa –

OTTOBAH. Rayowa? What did she call you?

VASSA. No. Stop –

OTTOBAH. What did she call you?

VASSA. Stop. I don't remember –

OTTOBAH. You do –

VASSA. I don't –

OTTOBAH. Remember. Try. Rayowa would call you...?

VASSA. I was supposed to look after her –

OTTOBAH. But she was taken?

VASSA. I tried –

OTTOBAH. What is your name? Come on, you couldn't protect her then and you're going to let her down again now?! What did she call you?

VASSA. I don't remember –

OTTOBAH. You do. What did she call you?

VASSA. Don't –

OTTOBAH. What did she call you?

VASSA. Please –

OTTOBAH. What did she call you?

VASSA. Don't remember –

AMA. Say it.

OTTOBAH. What did she call you?

VASSA. I don't know –

AMA. You do.

OTTOBAH. What did she call you?

VASSA. Ahhhhhh –

AMA. Say it.

OTTOBAH. What –

VASSA. I don't know. No! NO... I... She – Oh... OHH

OTTOBAH. What did she call you?

VASSA. OLAUDAH...

Time passes.

OTTOBAH. Olaudah. A true African name. Look at me, my brother. Olaudah. You are not to blame.

OLAUDAH. Her name –

OTTOBAH. There is power in her name.

OLAUDAH. I remember. Rayowa –

OTTOBAH. Rayowa, sister of…?

OLAUDAH. Olaudah. She is my family, and I don't know what happened to her. They took her. And my name was Olaudah Equiano –

OTTOBAH. Your name *is* Olaudah Equiano. Take it back.

A bang on the door.

GAOLER. Let's have you.

OTTOBAH. It is not your fault. Their lust is total. They are not satisfied with colonising our land. They seek to colonise our bodies, our minds, our thoughts, colonise our feelings, our talent, our culture. Our sense of self. Say you have a child with this woman. What can you tell your child? You are the father and you can tell him nothing because you do not know your own story. What do we tell our children? And a hundred years from now, when they are running about the streets lost and confused, how will we undo that? Slavery will end and when it does the whites will have to face whatever scars are left. But so will we.

OLAUDAH. When I read that newspaper I heard them, Oto. I heard my sister's voice. Every ship I see. Every one of us sold. I hear her.

OTTOBAH. Then answer. All our sisters are out there still. You have an opportunity tomorrow, Olaudah. What you heard was the calling.

'The Song of Unforgetting'.

AMA (*to* OLAUDAH). Speak your name.

OTTOBAH. For there is a calling on your life.

AMA (*to* OLAUDAH). None shall know Peace until there is Justice.

Scene Ten

Parliament Square.

Bells of the Abbey. Gulls. A passing carriage. ANNIE *approaches* GRANVILLE.

GRANVILLE. I did not expect to see you.

ANNIE. Clearly.

GRANVILLE. I should have told you. I owe you an apology.

ANNIE. And one shilling. After today – two.

GRANVILLE. You want to come back in?

ANNIE. You want this hearing documented because – ?

GRANVILLE. I wish the slave trade abolished.

ANNIE. Well, I am ashamed to say I knew so little of it but... so do I. Which side do you need to win?

GRANVILLE. I should like both sides to lose.

ANNIE. How do we achieve that?

GRANVILLE. This is the question.

OLAUDAH (*arriving*). Do you see us the same as horses?

GRANVILLE. Gustav. It's starting. Have you seen Pigott?

OLAUDAH. Miss Greenwood. Do you see us the same as horses?

ANNIE. Course not.

OLAUDAH (*to* GRANVILLE). You?

GRANVILLE. Would I be here if I did?

OLAUDAH. Do you see us the –

GRANVILLE. No.

OLAUDAH. Then you believe that we are equal?

GRANVILLE. We are all human.

OLAUDAH. But are we equal?

GRANVILLE. In God's eyes.

OLAUDAH. In your eyes?

GRANVILLE. I am sorry. Is that –

OLAUDAH. I don't need you to be sorry, I need you to be better.

ANNIE. You do both realise the hearing is about to resume?

GRANVILLE. I never said I was perfect.

OLAUDAH. You don't need to be perfect, Granville. How can we expect them to see those on that ship as human if we cannot be human ourselves? What is it to be human? To be imperfect. As Our Lord was. You study the grammar of the Bible but not the man? Be imperfect, flawed, wrong, real. Human. I cannot be brittle and neither must you be.

GRANVILLE. I see them as human beings who have the same right to justice as myself, Mansfield or anyone else. But in there it is not what we think that matters, but what they think.

ANNIE. 'If a man cannot insure his property then how would there be any trade?' That is what Sir John Lee thinks. He said it yesterday.

GRANVILLE *and* OLAUDAH *are puzzled.*

Do you have the book? (*Reads.*) 'If a man cannot insure his property then how would there be any trade?' I had no idea slaves were insured and I know little of the law but Mister Pigott also mentioned yesterday… a certain recommendation amongst the trade as to how many Africans ought safely to be on board any given ship per tonne.

GRANVILLE. Weskett's digest of laws and insurance practices. His point being that disease spread so quickly because of the excessive number of people on board.

ANNIE (*reads*). 'A ship of a hundred tonnes should house no more than three hundred.' Well then.

GRANVILLE. Well then what?

ANNIE. If you could reduce that figure…

OLAUDAH. How?

GRANVILLE. Parliamentary legislation –

ANNIE. If you could make it so that a ship of a hundred tonnes could only safely house not three hundred but, say, two hundred and fifty?

OLAUDAH. Or two hundred?

GRANVILLE. Or twenty.

ANNIE. It becomes impossible for ships to make their profit.

GRANVILLE. Death by legislation.

OLAUDAH. Change must come now. That takes a long time.

GRANVILLE. Not if we have the public with us. Legislation passes when the public is behind it.

OLAUDAH. This story must give us that support.

ANNIE. Only if we are in there to record it.

GRANVILLE. You'd make an effective lawyer, Mister Vassa.

OLAUDAH. My name is Olaudah Equiano. My father named me. He was an embrenche, which in Africa is a kind of judge.

Scene Eleven

A packed Westminster Hall.

CLERK. All rise.

MANSFIELD. Let justice be done though the heavens fall. Where is Mister Pigott?

CLERK. I don't know, excellency.

MANSFIELD. Go.

The CLERK *goes.*

LEE. Might I suggest we proceed and close?

PIGOTT (*runs in, breathless*). Forgive me, my lord.

MANSFIELD. There is no excuse for lateness, Mister Pigott.

PIGOTT. In this instance, my lord, I think you'll agree that there is. I have in my hand a signed statement from a witness which I believe will interest the court.

LEE. What witness?

PIGOTT (*holds up papers*). James Kelsall, first mate of *The Zong*.

The courtroom bristles.

GRANVILLE. My God.

OLAUDAH. He found him.

LEE. I object.

PIGOTT. If it please the court?

MANSFIELD. Where is the man?

PIGOTT. I located him last evening, my lord. He did not wish to appear but he agreed to a signed affidavit. Evidence disproving the slave traders' argument. My lord...?

Beat.

MANSFIELD. No. I don't think so. Be seated. And do not come late to my court again.

PIGOTT. What?!

GRANVILLE. Why not?

OLAUDAH. What is this?

LEE. I should like to continue with my closing, my lord.

MANSFIELD. Do.

PIGOTT. We must hear Kelsall's evidence.

OLAUDAH. It must be heard!!

ANNIE. Mister Vassa.

OLAUDAH. This must be heard.

MANSFIELD. Order! I'll not warn you again.

PIGOTT. My lord, these fellows are now advising me!

Everyone is stunned.

LEE. A Negro lawyer. Whatever next?

PIGOTT....This is perhaps the greatest case that ever came before this court. For we now not merely defend the underwriters from the damages obtained against them, we appear as council for millions of mankind and the cause of humanity in general.

OLAUDAH. None shall know Peace until there is Justice.

GRANVILLE. Gustavus, careful –

MANSFIELD. Silence! Sir John, proceed.

LEE. My lord, if a person insures slaves as property, they are thrown overboard from necessity as any other irrational or inanimate cargo might be, he is entitled to recover the cost.

OLAUDAH. Inanimate?!

GRANVILLE. My lord, the property in their persons is limited, I say, by the necessary consideration of their human –

MANSFIELD. Hold your tongue!

OLAUDAH. Animate!

LEE. It is law.

OLAUDAH. It is criminal.

MANSFIELD. I warn you.

GRANVILLE. The argument of the Solicitor General –

LEE. Anyone else's opinion that it is bad, tyrannical or wicked is irrelevant. These were property.

OLAUDAH. PROPERTY!?

MANSFIELD. Put that man out!

OLAUDAH. There! You said it. Man. Not property.

GRANVILLE. Not chattels.

OLAUDAH. Man!

ANNIE. Just as those on *The Zong* were men and women.

OLAUDAH. 'I wish some man of feeling would give poetic
language to one of those brave fellow's thoughts! I wish
some man of feeling would give poetic language to one of
those brave fellow's thoughts!'

*The building begins to SHUDDER. A dreadful rumbling. The
sound grows. Something hurtling towards us at an incredible
speed. The walls shake.*

I am Olaudah Equiano. Olaudah meaning: *One who speaks
well* or *One with a loud voice*!

A shattering spasm of light, deafening noise, and The Zong
*smashes through the stained-glass St Stephen's window into
Westminster Hall. The court is irrevocably changed.*

RIBA, AMA *and* JOYI *step from the deck of* The Zong,
*resplendent in their Ancestral aura, and address the court
and audience.*

AMA. I am Ama. One of one hundred and thirty-two. One of
four hundred and sixty-two. One of twelve million who built
this country. Hear us.

MANSFIELD....The court will hear Colonel Kelsall's evidence.

AMA (*to us, pointing at* PIGOTT). He tells you what happened.

RIBA. We show you what happened.

JOYI. You decide.

   PIGOTT *reads* KELSALL*'s affidavit.*

PIGOTT/KELSALL. 'I, James Kelsall, in October 1780 did
purchase on behalf of Mister Gregson a small slave ship
sitting at port and embark on a Business of Trade across to
Jamaica aboard this *The Zong*.'

And we are on the deck of The Zong.

'One hundred endless days. Captain Collingwood too sick to
command. Sees fit to replace me with Mister Stubbs. Four
crew dead, including the second mate. November 29th errors

are discovered, the remaining crew are called on deck and
we discuss the situation like gentlemen.'

STUBBS. Well whose job was it?!

MICHAEL. Water barrels are nothing to do with me!

GEORGE. You're the one supposed to man 'em!

STUBBS. You sure they've leaked?

GEORGE. Yes! (*At* MICHAEL.) Or someone's been thieving it.

MICHAEL (*goes for him*). Fuck off!

STUBBS. Right, listen up!!

KELSALL (*arriving*). Thank you, Mister Stubbs. Now, men –

STUBBS. Excuse me, Mister Kelsall, I'm handling this.

KELSALL. I'm reinstated now, Mister Stubbs –

STUBBS. Says who?

KELSALL. Captain Collingwood.

STUBBS. Over my dead body –

KELSALL. Have it your way. (*To the crew*.) LISTEN UP!
Captain is worse and has been informed that the water butts
have leaked. There's more. It has been brought to my
attention that we are in fact now leeward of Jamaica.

MICHAEL. What?

GEORGE. I knew it!

KELSALL. By some three hundred miles.

JOHN. We're dead.

KELSALL. Silence!! With these winds it'll take us eleven days
to get back, and we have only three days' water left. Now, if
we work we can make it.

STUBBS. Go back? Why? Head for the nearest island.

KELSALL. We're going back.

GEORGE. We've missed the Jamaica slave market as it is. Stock'll be worthless by the time we get there! It's all right for you, we get paid out the profits.

KELSALL. So do I!

MICHAEL. What do we do then?!

JOHN. Who's in charge of this fucking ship?

KELSALL. Me.

STUBBS. Me.

GEORGE. I say we'd do a better job.

KELSALL. Watch your mouth, boy.

GEORGE. What do we do then?!!

STUBBS. Throw 'em in.

Silence.

MICHAEL. Who?

STUBBS. Who d'you think? Them lot down there's sucking up your water and giving you their disease.

GEORGE. The fuck do you know? You got us in this mess.

STUBBS. I know them wogs are worth more to you in the sea than on this ship.

JOHN. You mad?! That's our cargo.

STUBBS. Which is insured. (*To* KELSALL.) Is it not?

Beat.

KELSALL. He's right.

JOHN. So?

STUBBS. Think about it. Keep 'em on board –

KELSALL. – They drink our water. Swallow our wages.

STUBBS. Throw 'em in –

KELSALL. The insurer pays. We keep our water, reach Jamaica, and you'll have wages when you get back home.

STUBBS. And the owners'll give you big fat kiss for turning
'em a profit.

Pause.

MICHAEL. I'm in.

GEORGE. I don't trust him.

KELSALL. Collingwood would have to authorise it.

STUBBS. Thought you was in charge. He'll be dead as a brick
by dawn.

BROWN. Throw them in? Alive you mean? We mustn't.

MICHAEL. Must.

GEORGE (*to* KELSALL). Sir?

STUBBS. Course, if you wanna be a failure cunt all your life...

JOHN. Sir...?

Pause.

KELSALL. We vote.

A single low drum begins under –

Each man must give his consent or dissent. Michael Sullivan?
John Barnes? George Aston? Elijah Brown?... Elijah Brown??

BROWN (*shaking his head, unable to speak, he finally finds the
words*). For what doth it profit a man to gain the whole world
and forfeit his soul?

KELSALL. Majority. It is decided. About your task. Women
and children first.

Drum under –

OLAUDAH. forty-six thirty-six forty ten

AMA. forty-six

OLAUDAH. thirty-six

GRANVILLE. forty

ANNIE. ten

Scene Twelve

Split scene. KELSALL *in court, and* AMA *and* JOYI *pleading with* RIBA.

KELSALL. The second evening, something strange happened.

AMA (*to* RIBA). Auntie, talk to him –

JOYI (*to* RIBA). Make them stop –

KELSALL. From the darkness I heard a voice call my name.

AMA. Go –

KELSALL. One of the Africans somehow spoke English.

AMA. Speak for us –

RIBA. Let me think –

AMA. No time to think. They are coming –

JOYI. Then speak to our ancestors.

AMA. They can help us. Someone is trying to help us and they can light his way –

JOYI. No one is coming. Riba, you must be Okomfo.

RIBA. I have not those gifts.

JOYI. Your mother was Okomfo. Could see things and talk to God.

RIBA. I am not my mother –

JOYI. Call them!

RIBA. With what?

ANNIE (*in court*). Did she sit? Stand? Naked or covered?

AMA. Tell them to stop.

RIBA. Stop.

AMA. You know better?

ANNIE. Did she wear a ring? Could she cook? Did she have a favourite colour?

JOYI. There are Abasom in the waters, are there not?

RIBA. Yes.

JOYI. And they could not bear our brothers and sisters up and save them?

RIBA. Such things may be beyond the Abasom –

ANNIE. Could she smile? Count? Did she ever love? Children?

JOYI. Perhaps the white men have their god in the ocean and we are their sacrifice to him. I heard that they have a god who walks upon the waters.

ANNIE. Could she swim? Was she elected? If she could speak, could she spell? Could she write? What could she write?

AMA. Speak to them!

RIBA. Shh –

JOYI. I hear them –

RIBA. Where?

JOYI. There.

AMA. Ha?!

RIBA. Shh – (*Beat*.) I will talk to him.

KELSALL. The sound persisted and though now down to our last lamp I went… She appealed to me. I listened and calmed them.

Scene Thirteen

The hold of The Zong.

RIBA (*to* KELSALL). Please. Stop killing us. The water is low. We know. We ask for no water or food.

We will live without till we reach.

Please stop. Please. Mister Kelsall. Stop killing us. Stop killing us. Why do you do this? You don't have to do this.

A moment, then –

KELSALL (*suddenly exploding*). Take your fucking eyes off
   me. Don't you look at me. What, spare you and throw the
   rest, that it? Because you're special? Because you speak my
   language? Fuck you. You're trying to save yourself just as I
   am. So don't plead to me, plead to God. You're His problem
   now. When I come back you'll have water enough. You
   decide which one of you. (*Pushes her back into the hold*.)

   RIBA *returns to the* WOMEN.

AMA. What did he say?

RIBA. He's coming back. To take one of us.

JOYI. In the ocean?

AMA. Nooooo –

JOYI. Which one?

AMA. Not me.

JOYI. He did not come for me. (*To* RIBA.) You.

RIBA. What? Do not look at me –

AMA. The white man favours you –

RIBA. I've seen him look at *you* –

AMA. You angered him –

RIBA. You told me to go!

JOYI (*to* AMA). You are Anyi. The Anyi have caused this –

AMA. You are sick. You should go. I am young –

JOYI. So am I. You should die –

RIBA. None of us will go! We are sisters. We too have gods.
   (*Beat*.) My mother had a drum.

JOYI. Yes –

AMA. Remember, Auntie –

RIBA. We have none –

AMA. We will drum. Come. (*She taps her two fingers on the wooden floor*.)

RIBA. My mother would call on Asase Yaa. First we must offer –

AMA. The chains –

RIBA. We cannot enslave our spirits as these white men have tried to enslave us –

AMA. Hair. Reach and take a piece –

JOYI. Wait, this is not the way. We do it differently. First we must sing –

AMA. No. First we must offer.

RIBA. We are calling on the same source. Place it. And sing. I will try.

> AMA *takes a piece of hair from* JOYI'*s head*.

> RIBA *speaks some words slowly. Trying to remember. The ship lurches*.

> Drum.

> *The* WOMEN *drum with their fingers*. RIBA *closes her eyes*. JOYI *starts*. AMA *joins*. RIBA *begins to move as a rhythm is established*. RIBA *hums as she sways, whispering the words to a fragment of song/prayer. She stretches and tries to hold her hand over the hair*.

> An offer of libation?

JOYI. Tears.

> *She gestures to* AMA, *who stretches up and places her finger at her eyes and then places her fingertip down next to the hair*.

> Accept them.

> *Deeper, faster movement. Then suddenly* JOYI *is very still*.

RIBA. What do you want?

> AMA *and* JOYI *look to each other*.

JOYI....Okomfo? Please, we are in great danger –

AMA. Harm is being done us –

JOYI. They are killing us –

The drumming grows stronger.

AMA. They have taken us –

JOYI. Chained us –

AMA. How shall we free ourselves?

JOYI. They hurt us. One of the murder men he, he, he, please, he... He comes to me, smiles – says words to me in his language that I do not understand, but I know he means me to be still and make no noise. I feel as if I'm tearing inside and I hope that no one will see. I pretend that I am home with my mother up in the ground, but I feel sick because I know that her heart would break if she could see what this white man is doing to her child.

AMA. Please. Show us some sign –

JOYI. My grandmother said a girl is the one who has questions and a woman is the one who has answers. But I cannot answer why this is happening to us. Now I have pains. Please –

RIBA. I... I...

JOYI. The men are dead.

AMA. Show us some sign?

JOYI. Please. We must bury our brothers and sisters. This is sacred.

JOYI. Help us. Carry us from the storms of death back to our peaceful ways –

AMA. Please. Our mothers are waiting on us –

RIBA. I... I... –

JOYI. Please –

AMA. Please.

JOYI. Please. Speak to us –

AMA. Come to us –

JOYI. Please. They are coming –

AMA. Please.

JOYI. Please.

AMA. Tear these chains off our hands and those cold hands from off our bodies –

AMA. That by and by we might look up and see –

AMA *and* JOYI. Home. (*Beat.*) Auntie??!!

   – as RIBA, *exhausted, collapses.*

RIBA....I can't... I can't. I'm sorry.

   There is a noise at the door. The silhouette of KELSALL.

PIGOTT. Is this thing to be justified? The life of one man is like the life of another whatever his colour. I contend that that thimble full of water, if it were no more, these men and women have as good a right as the captain or any man on that ship. Kelsall goes on –

KELSALL. All told half the people who left Africa died. Six crew. One mate. Two hundred and four Africans. Two hundred and three I should say, for one of the Africans that was thrown into the sea did somehow manage to catch hold of a rope hanging from the ship and there clung on with her bare hands –

   The entire stage is suddenly bare. Drums ring out. A rope swings down from above, stage-right. From stage-left AMA *runs out. She grabs for the rope as she passes it centre of the stage. Misses. She runs back as the rope swings back to the right. She lunges for it – misses again. On the third pass she launches herself and grabs hold. Swinging, struggling to breathe and hold on in the vast churning ocean.*

AMA. Terror
  Let loose
  In waves
  Tides of sulphur
  Life on fire
  Gusts of ice.

  Joyi??!

Riba??!!

Blood and Chaos
What world is this? Help! Hear. Hold.

The waves throw her.

Breathe. Salt. Breathe. Bodies. Arms, clawing at clouds.

Wilderness of sea. Raw red

Frothing with limbs and chains and the ferocious fish begin
to feed on us even as we die.
Storm Ama storm

Breathe girl
Battlefield of open mouths

Ecstasy of blood
God... why is this happening? Cannot breathe... Cannot
swim
One man, Ashanti – straight down
Others – a blur of digits... foam... foul... spurts of blood.
Help me!
Men heads – now pulp
God? Am I going to die?
Storm Ama storm

Drums blare as the ocean crashes around her –

Help me
O God.

A huge wave smashes her –

My arm reaches out the water like a weed, grabbing for ship.
Hold firm the rope.

*The rope pulls away from her. The drums and flute flare with
the howling wind –*

God

Another wave.

Little as I am hear me.

Another wave.

Gasp at the choking moon – swallow a bleeding ocean.

Another wave. She struggles to hold.

No!

The rope suddenly flies out of her hand.

No no no no no!

Rope cracks – whips away – Ship away. Rope away. Hope
away.
NO!!

She grabs for the rope.

No! Snake! Catch the snake. (*Flings herself forward.*)
Throw my mouth towards rope.
Feet bucking beneath like a newborn foal.
Less than a speck I wrestle the flow.
A broken arm's length between me and my rope.

Thighs run hills of sea. Divinity, where are you? You make a
bitter dancer of me. Chop crops of waves. A frayed finger's
length. Manmaker – the sea – unspleening me. Does this
matter not matter to you? If you hear – answer. If you care –
come.

Waves smash her. She blacks out for a second.

…Is this rope in my hand? (*It is. She cannot breathe.*) This
dream – not good. Rope, yesterday I saw fish that fly. Ha ha.
Well, if birds can swim – may fish not fly? Were I a flying
fish… Rope, perhaps God has been round the tree of
forgetting also. Bear with me, rope. Rough. Battered. But
here. Made for human hands. Hands – Hands – This hand is
brown – yet it will hold as well. The earth earth earth is
brown. Palm pink. What am I? Girl or water? Water or rope?
Rope in hand. This is my hand hand hand – My rope – At
each end – Death, with the big eyes. (*She clings on.*) O. I am
in the mines of my mind.

Threshing – behind. Screams. Shark rips the baby – baby
wails – water rushes in greedy for a host – reach out my
hand – waves pile on and where there was once a baby –
now only bloody foam

WHY? God – you murder.
You are at your sport.

Why have you turned against me?

Abandoned us

We called out to you and you did not come

Riba never harmed you. Nor Joyi nor her unborn child

You would destroy three poor women and yet allow those
butchers up there to live? This is your law? Then here are my
terms... WAR! Ahhh – Shark... return to your God – tell him
go to hell. Tell your bastard master I hate him! Tell him if he
dare show his bloodless face here I'd drown him dead – I'll
drown him dead, skin him, gut the carcass and piss on the
mess! For hate's sake. If he must stay silent I will give him
reason!

A terrible impact sound.

The sea roars. I am thrown at the sky. Then down I come as
wet rag and in a stroke under I go –

BOOM! The entire theatre is plunged into total darkness.
The music changes.

The waters compassed me about even to the soul.

Gradually as she speaks light emerges from the dark and
floods the theatre. The rope is gone. We are underwater.

Light.
Colour.
I hear colours.
Black
White
Yellow
Brown
Red
Far from the Great Fish now. From Riba. From Joyi. From
Rope. Now I am alone.

Looks around her.

Swim. Strange.

I told my mother I would not be long gone. Riba… Joyi… I am SORRY.

She is totally alone. Exhausted.

God?

O God

You gave me my life…

and now

you take it

She sinks in the water. She is being pulled further and further and further down. She sits, closes her eyes. Sings very simply –

Tue tue barima due due Abofra ba Ama wa da wa

Due due –

Suddenly from the depths we see a figure approach. It is OLAUDAH.

You!

OLAUDAH. You. I have been where you are.

AMA. In the depths.

OLAUDAH. So low,

AMA. So lost,

OLAUDAH. So lonely that I could not see a way. We cannot always see the *why*. They took my sister from me. And I did not know why. Why a thing happens is not the question, rather *what we do* when a thing happens.

AMA. Not the reason –

OLAUDAH. The response. She was like you. Always wanted to know why. Why fire was hot, I said – it's hot because it's hot, the thing is whether you let it burn you or light your way. She wanted to know why the river was deep, I said – it's deep because it is, the thing is whether you sink in it or swim. You are like her. But I know she fought.

AMA. Did not give up.

OLAUDAH. Did not let go. And neither will you.

AMA. You cannot stay here.

OLAUDAH. You must go back. Not the reason –

AMA. The response.

OLAUDAH. You are not my sister but you are –

OLAUDAH *take the chains from* AMA *and they fall slowly away. She rises up in the water, childlike. Turning over and over in the colours of the water. Music. She dances through the abyss. Observes* OLAUDAH, *who is going.*

AMA. Thank you –

An enormous tear, a spasm of light, AMA *is rocked by a shuddering gasp as her head comes russsshing to the surface of the water. Her eyes wide, she choke/gasp/splutters in the cold Atlantic night air. Rope is in her hand. Shivering, she bobs. The ships bell tolls four. When she can, she speaks.*

God… I am a woman. No more, no less. I could not see that that which looked to me a rope was in truth a finger on your outstretched hand.

Gripping the rope. The first spot of light in the corner of the sky. She looks directly at The Zong.

You can throw me into the sea a million times… I will climb back out. Tomorrow I will be here again. Do you understand me? The day after that I will be here again. And again. And again. And again. Throw me to Death once more and I will climb back out. Emerge. From the horizon I will come. You cannot kill me. For I will pull myself up from the jaws of Death and once more see the sun of a new day. I will keep coming. God will lift me, or I will elevate myself, but I will rise. I will rise. I will rise. I will rise. The sun rises and I rise too.

I live.

Scene Fourteen

Westminster Hall.

GRANVILLE. These were not three-headed creatures who
   committed these crimes. These were ordinary men. The men
   one sits next to every Sunday morning. Brought to murder
   under the law.

ANNIE. In Westminster Hall men talk of horrors as the morning
   sun streams in and I write it down. My ink begins to run low.
   In the bottles blue – the faces Pigott speaks of appear to me.

Scene Fifteen

The hold of The Zong.

RIBA *and* JOYI *sit in the dark hold*. JOYI *– sicker now.*

JOYI. Riba? The sun is here.

RIBA. Almost. Hold on.

JOYI. By and by. Ama is gone. I am next.

RIBA. I will be as one of the dead. When he comes I will throw
   them – (*Re: the chains*.) around his neck. When he is dead
   take the key, go straight to the men's cabin. We will take this
   ship and go home.

JOYI. Mister, go. Go away from here.

RIBA. Shhh. There is no one here.

JOYI. You have a sweet voice, Riba… You are wrong.

RIBA. Look at me.

JOYI. Go away, mister – By and by.

RIBA. We must walk from off this ship. We are women. We
   walk. With proud hips and children on our backs. Water on
   our heads. Not beneath our feet.

We are linked… to each other. We must be subject not to the
chains which we see but the ones we do not. For the ties
which bind us one to the other have been in place since
before these oceans rolled and make steel seem as straw.

JOYI. Riba? Give me a story –

RIBA. Not now –

JOYI. Yes. Like the ones you tell to teach the young ones when
we first came on this boat… Plait my hair and tell me the
story. I am dying. (*She closes her eyes, puts her head on*
RIBA*'s lap.*)

RIBA. Anansi?

JOYI. Anansi.

RIBA (*knows what she has to do*). Spider Anansi decided to
take all the wisdom of the world for himself. He's clever,
Anansi, but he thought, 'You know I should have all the
wisdom.' So, he took his wife's biggest cooking pot –

JOYI. She would be vexed –

RIBA. Mmmhmm – and he grabbed up all the wisdom in the
world, but he didn't know where to hide it. So next night he
crept deep into the forest and climbed the tallest ginkgo tree.
His son, Ntikuma, saw him go and followed.

But the pot was too big for Anansi to hold and climb, so he
tied it to his belly. But the pot kept getting in the way and
butting the tree and Anansi kept slipping down. He cursed,
saying –

RIBA *and* JOYI. 'What's wrong with this pot!? What's wrong
with this tree?'

RIBA. Ntikuma laughed. 'I don't know why you don't tie the
pot on your back, Father, you could skin up the tree better.'
Anansi was so mad when he realised that the child was right
that the calabash slipped out of his hands, smashed on the
ground and all the wisdom spilled. A storm blew up and the
sweet rains washed the wisdom into the river, all out into the
sea, to every corner of the world, so that now everybody has
a piece of wisdom.

JOYI *breaths shallowly.*

JOYI. Riba?

RIBA. Yes?

JOYI. You take my wisdom... use it wisely... By and by – And next time you tell a story... please tell mine... my child –

Go, go from here, mister –
...Go...

She lets go her final breath...

Silence.

RIBA *sings gently.*

The ship bell tolls five. Silence. RIBA *starts. She has heard something.*

A sound above her head. She prepares herself. Again there is the sound. Tap... Another tap. Another. Two. Three. More. Something hitting the wood above her head. The sound of tapping all around her. Covering the deck. A million tiny taps. Faster and faster. Louder. A driving rhythm. She listens in amazement as the sound grows all around her. The entire ship, wooden and hollow, becomes one vast drum as the heavens open, the deluge comes on and the vessel vibrates under the din. In the sound are Fante rhythms, Yoruba rhythms, Ashanti rhythms. Islam and Anyi rhythms. The beats rise around RIBA. *She looks up as drips now begin to come through the beams. With them the first rays of daylight. She tilts her head, opens her mouth and drinks. Lapping the water. The whole theatre is ringing. A ferocious pounding rhythm all around, smashing the entire ship.*

She raises her head and arms to the sound. In the courtroom OLAUDAH *begins to pound his fists on the table as loudly as he can.* ANNIE *joins in, beating on the table loudly with the rhythm. Finally* GRANVILLE *joins them, smashing his fists on the wooden table with the others. The audience join in and the whole ship/theatre shudders violently, hammered by the rain. The sound climaxes as* RIBA *can take no more and suddenly all is still –*

RIBA *slowly opens her eyes and sees... a shadow at the end of the hold. It becomes a figure as it moves closer, out of the shadows. Staggering. It is* AMA. *Sodden. Shivering. Bloodied.* RIBA *is shaking.* AMA *raises her finger to her lips.* RIBA *faintly shakes her head.* AMA *even more faintly nods hers. Takes a step towards the* WOMEN. RIBA *stretches out her hand as if to touch what has appeared in front of her.* AMA *lifts her arm and slowly takes hold of* RIBA*'s hand.* RIBA *struggles to come to one knee. Then stands. Her hand reaches up and touches* AMA*'s wet hair. The sound of rain.*

AMA. I come from a land where the mountains are Great, the animals Strong and the people Ancient...

As the image holds KELSALL *steps forward.*

KELSALL. The weather turned, the last lamp was dowsed, the oil gone, I was unable to take the readings and we were in darkness until we reached Black River two weeks later.

Scene Sixteen

Westminster Hall.

MANSFIELD *cuts through.*

MANSFIELD. 'Dowsed'?! (*Checks his papers, confused.*) According to this – did not the encounter between Kelsall and the Negress who pleaded with him take place on the evening... December 1st?

LEE. My lord...?

MANSFIELD. That exchange took place on December 1st?

LEE. Possibly, I don't see... (*Leafs through his notes.*)

OLAUDAH. Meaning the last lamp was also extinguished on December 1st?

GRANVILLE. The second night of killings.

MANSFIELD. That night rain fell?!

LEE. I think not. Here it says in fact –

PIGOTT (*grabs and reads from the testimony*). That is correct, my lord. Kelsall's testimony continues: 'At least we had caught some few gallons which sustained the crew till we arrived in Black River.'

The courtroom stirs.

ANNIE. Caught.

OLAUDAH. Between the devil and the deep blue sea.

GRANVILLE. Dear God.

MANSFIELD. And yet?

OLAUDAH. The rains came on that night, December 1st, and yet...

KELSALL. 'On December 2nd a *third* parcel of thirty-six more slaves were gathered and thrown into the sea. The number drowned in all being one hundred and thirty-two. I do in conscience believe the throwing overboard of the Africans an act of absolute necessity to preserve the lives of the slaves and crew from perishing for *want of water*.'

PIGOTT. They lied about the number of Africans on board, their navigational errors, the water supply *and* the location of the logbook which would expose every one of their crimes. Is it too much to conjure that it too was thrown into the sea?

GRANVILLE. They've blamed each other and the elements, but what is certain is that none of these acts could have taken place without the sanction of the ship's owners. William Gregson and his trade are responsible for these murders.

PIGOTT. There was no necessity. How could there ever have been? For to say that wantonly or by ignorance a captain may drown one hundred and thirty-two people is a proposition that shocks humanity. A deed so wicked, were it to be perpetuated to future generations it would not be believed. But believed it must be and when we tell them let

us make them understand that it was the British slave trade
which occasioned it. And any jury who favours this massacre
by their judgment against my clients must be considered as
abettors in the guilt of all murders of the same kind
promoted by these events.

As you have said many times in many courts, my lord – let
justice be done... though the heavens fall.

MANSFIELD. Sir John?

LEE. British law must be observed here, my lord, for if it is not
then it hardly calls for me to say that the consequences of such
negligence on our part must surely come on to sink us all.

MANSFIELD. The question put to us is whether this was an act
of absolute necessity, and whether sufficient evidence exists
for the case to be reheard.

(*Looking through his papers*.) The cause of delay does not
appear the same as that stated in the declaration. (*Beat*.)
There is weight also, in the circumstances of the throwing
overboard more Negroes... after the rain, which upon the
evidence there appears to have been no necessity.

It is this court's decision... therefore... that... there should
be a new trial on pain of costs. Court dismissed.

COURT CLERK. All rise!

Over which –

OLAUDAH. forty-six

RIBA. thirty-six

JOYI. forty

AMA. ten

OLAUDAH. one hundred and thirty-two

Scene Seventeen

Parliament Square.

COMPANY. Outside the hall, pounding the pavement –

COMPANY. Our heroes pursue the end of enslavement –

OLAUDAH. Whether another trial ever took place we do not know but we left Westminster Hall with a narrative.

GRANVILLE. Gustav, the African who speaks out and the African who holds out. We organise and campaign in their names. They instruct us.

OLAUDAH. It was she who told me to come to your door. And, Granville, my name is Olaudah.

GRANVILLE. Olaudah.

ANNIE (*to* OLAUDAH). Your father would be proud.

GRANVILLE. As would your brother.

ANNIE. Now this – (*Tapping her case.*) must go viral.

The CLERK *walks up.*

CLERK. Madam. May I have that book?

ANNIE. Excuse me?

CLERK. Their lordships request that document.

ANNIE. Why? It's mine.

CLERK. Madam?

GRANVILLE. That book is my property.

ANNIE. I wrote it.

GRANVILLE. I bought it.

ANNIE. But not the ink.

CLERK. It belongs to the court.

GRANVILLE (*takes the book*). This book belongs to me and whoever thinks otherwise I shall see in court, but rest assured, it comes with me.

CLERK (*holds out his hand*). Miss.

ANNIE, *to their horror hands over the book and the* CLERK *hurries off.*

GRANVILLE. Do you realise what you just did? You give away –

ANNIE. Absolutely nothing. Unsure if you'd let me join you today, I brought a book of my own. So, yes, I fully realise what I just did was give away a book full of empty pages. This, however... (*Producing* GRANVILLE's *book from her satchel.*) All of which I suspect they shall discover in the next two minutes. So I suggest we move. You're welcome.

GRANVILLE (*takes the book*). Thank you.

OLAUDAH. The book goes with you? Doesn't sound equal to me.

GRANVILLE. Very well, let us tear the pages out and divide them three ways. That would be equal. Or. We could meet at my house in the morning and work together. Because this cannot be read without you, it's your shorthand. It cannot be interpreted without my knowledge of the law and it cannot be taken out into the world without you. Equal does not mean same. Change is different people leaning to a common cause. People who might not look alike but who feel alike. Might not sound alike but think alike. This is where I failed. I've spent my life marching alone. Come tomorrow. We have work to do. (*Goes.*)

OLAUDAH (*to* ANNIE). He thinks I did not notice he still took the book.

ANNIE. He thinks I did not notice he left without paying me.

OLAUDAH. In the future people will know of this because of you.

ANNIE. Us, Mister Vassa – (*Correcting herself.*) Olaudah. (*Turns.*) I liked Mister Vassa. Do not be too hard on him. Farewell. Until tomorrow. (*Goes.*)

OLAUDAH. He still took the book.

AMA. Not the reason, the response.

OLAUDAH. After all that, he has the book.

AMA. But not the story. A story is not paper and ink. You are the story.

OLAUDAH. So?

AMA. You are a young Black man. You can do all things.

OTTOBAH *bowls up, accompanied by* WOODFALL.

OTTOBAH. I am looking for the Lord High Chief Justice Superintendent Badass Equiano. Lawyer man! Case winner! Emancipator. Imperialist slayer. I heard the news. You are coming to eat with us! I believe you know this man, or he knows you –

WOODFALL. William Woodfall.

OLAUDAH. Oh. We'd heard –

OTTOBAH. These fools lock the wrong people up together. We've been talking all morning, Olu.

WOODFALL. We shouldn't stay here but I understand you are all looking to get a paper or a pamphlet going. You'll need help. The insurers won this appeal but you won't get another trial. They'll settle out of court. Fudge.

OLAUDAH. It's too late. What was heard in that court can never be unheard, Oto. Now *we* have the narrative. I know now what I must do.

Scene Eighteen

The bookshop, present day.

GLORIA. What did you do?

OLAUDAH. I wrote my own story. My book. My truth. *The Interesting Narrative of the Life of Olaudah Equiano, Or Gustavus Vassa, the African.* They've got it over there, next to where you found that book.

GLORIA. On the –

BOTH. Wrong shelf.

OLAUDAH. Published it myself I'll have you know. The first to do it. I changed Britain, as you will. You come from strong people. Write your truth but make sure you live it.

TANNOY ANNOUNCEMENT. Ladies and gentlemen, the shop is now closed. Please make your way to the exits. Thank you.

GLORIA. Yeah.

OLAUDAH. Don't wait for them.

GLORIA. Write my own story...

OLAUDAH. And then you tell them where it belongs.

ACTOR WHO PLAYED RIBA (*to us*). Olaudah's book, the world's first so-called Slave Narrative, is hugely successful. He takes it throughout Britain, highlighting the injustice of Britain's slave trade. He and Ottobah join members of London's extensive Black community to form the abolitionist Sons of Africa Committee. While Granville, Thomas Clarkson, William Wilberforce form the Society for Effecting the Abolition of the Slave Trade. The world's first human rights organisations.

ACTOR WHO PLAYED GRANVILLE. That same year Prime Minister William Pitt moves a resolution in Parliament to consider the circumstances of the slave trade.

ACTOR WHO PLAYED OTTOBAH. Eight years later, in 1807, Parliament passes the Abolition of the Slave Trade Act.

ACTOR WHO PLAYED JOYI. In 1833, slavery itself is abolished in British colonies.

ACTOR WHO PLAYED MANSFIELD. Though, the abolition act contains provisions for the financial compensation of former British slave-owning families by the British taxpayer to the tune of sixteen billion pounds –

ACTOR WHO PLAYED OLAUDAH. The largest bailout in British history until the 2008 banking crisis.

ACTOR WHO PLAYED ANNIE. *The Zong* campaign does succeed in igniting the idea of international human rights.

ACTOR WHO PLAYED PIGOTT. The retrial of *The Zong* case can be heard every day then.

ACTOR WHO PLAYED STUBBS. At Nuremberg.

ACTOR WHO PLAYED MANSFIELD. In South Africa's Truth and Reconciliation Commission.

ACTOR WHO PLAYED RIBA. International Criminal Tribunal for Yugoslavia.

ACTOR WHO PLAYED OTTOBAH. Rwanda.

ACTOR WHO PLAYED JOYI. Hamdan vs Rumsfeld.

ACTOR WHO PLAYED GRANVILLE. The Macpherson Report.

ACTOR WHO PLAYED ANNIE. Grenfell Tower.

ACTOR WHO PLAYED AMA. At borders across Europe, and on overcrowded boats in the Mediterranean and the English Channel.

ACTOR WHO PLAYED LEE. In the struggles of the over twenty million human beings trapped in sex trafficking, forced labour and child labour today.

ACTOR WHO PLAYED GRANVILLE. – And what of the African who held on to the rope? Kelsall states:

ACTOR WHO PLAYED KELSALL. They were discovered next morning and kept on board.

ACTOR WHO PLAYED ANNIE. After that?

ACTOR WHO PLAYED AMA. Who knows? But I like to think that she made it to dry land and lived and lived and lived. She is Me.

ACTOR WHO PLAYED OLAUDAH. Therefore we come in honour of all those who dare to stand up in the face of many dangers, to the twelve million human beings who lost their lives to the transatlantic slave trade holocaust, and finally to those of you who survived to walk from those ships.

ALL. Peace.

The End.

www.nickhernbooks.co.uk

facebook.com/nickhernbooks

twitter.com/nickhernbooks